STEPHEN PLATTEN
Stephen Platten is Bishop of Wakefi
Theological College. Later he was
Secretary for Ecumenical Affairs before becoming Dean of Norwich
in 1995. Stephen is the author of *Pilgrims* and *Augustine's Legacy*, and
is the author and editor of several other books. He has recently been
appointed Chairman of the Liturgical Commission.

CHRISTOPHER LEWIS
Christopher Lewis is Dean of Christ Church, Oxford. He has worked
in two other cathedrals: St Albans as Dean, and Canterbury as a
residentiary canon. Before ordination, he spent five years in the
Royal Navy. After a first degree at Bristol and Ph.D. at Cambridge,
he taught theology at Ripon College, Cuddesdon, and was Vicar of
Spalding.

DREAMING SPIRES?

Cathedrals in a New Age

Edited by
Stephen Platten and Christopher Lewis

First published in Great Britain in 2006

Society for Promoting Christian Knowledge
36 Causton Street
London SW1P 4ST

British Library Cataloguing-in-Publication Data
A catalogue record for this book is available from the British Library

ISBN-13: 978–0–281–05667–5
ISBN-10: 0–281–05667–6

1 3 5 7 9 10 8 6 4 2

Typeset by Graphicraft Limited, Hong Kong
Printed in Great Britain by Bookmarque

For
Alan Webster and Hugh Dickinson,
who have lived out their dreams in cathedrals

Contents

————•◆•————

Contents

Contributors

The Very Revd James Atwell – Dean of Winchester

Professor Grace Davie – Director, the Centre for European Studies at the University of Exeter

The Revd Canon Jeremy Fletcher – Canon Precentor, York Minster

The Rt Revd John Inge – Bishop of Huntingdon

The Rt Revd Graham James – Bishop of Norwich

Ms Jane Kennedy – Architect and Surveyor of Fabrics to Ely Cathedral

The Very Revd Christopher Lewis – Dean of Christ Church Oxford

The Rt Revd Stephen Platten – Bishop of Wakefield

The Very Revd Michael Sadgrove – Dean of Durham

Mr Philip Thomas – Assistant Cathedral Archaeologist, Norwich Cathedral

1

Introduction – dreaming spires?

STEPHEN PLATTEN

Dreams or visions?

In his recent book on cathedral deans, Trevor Beeson writes:

> 'Flagships of the spirit', 'Shopwindows of the Church of England', 'Supermarkets of religion'. These are just three of the descriptions of England's cathedrals coined by their deans during recent years . . . the descriptions point to the reforming zeal that radically altered the life of the cathedrals during the second half of the twentieth century. It is a transformation that many of the deans whose lives are chronicled in this book would have found incredible, though some would have enthusiastically approved, and their astonishment would have been heightened by the discovery that the revival of cathedral life took place during a period when the rest of the Church was in serious numerical and financial decline. There is nothing comparable in any other part of Western Europe.[1]

These words, from Beeson's brief lives of 22 deans (almost entirely of cathedrals) over the past 150 years, set the scene both for these introductory reflections and also for the parameters of this book. Some seven years ago now, during the time of the implementation of the Howe Report[2] on the cathedrals of the Church of England, a number of writers from both within and outside cathedral communities reflected on the role that cathedrals play within contemporary society.[3] The aim of that volume was to stimulate further debate and to encourage those responsible for cathedrals to explore new and imaginative ways of living out their contemporary role. This present volume aims to take that debate on one stage further, and Beeson's reflection offers a challenging starting point. In those few lines and elsewhere, both in his introductory and concluding chapters, Beeson demonstrates the revolution that has taken place. The nineteenth-century picture of English cathedrals was one of moribund white elephants collapsing in upon themselves through the sheer weight of tradition and inertia. One and a half centuries on, and cathedrals are found to be in a better state of conservation, and visited by more people, than ever before. Part of this is due (as Beeson suggests) to an energy for reform and a real sense of vision. The *dreaming spires* (and towers) of cathedrals have moved on from being merely the objects of poetic contemplation, as Matthew Arnold's lines on Oxford's skyline reflect. They have become places where people might *dream* or, better, *pursue a vision* for new models of Christian mission within the contemporary world – that stands at the heart of the title of this book.

Our subtitle addresses some of the key issues raised in the chapters that follow. If, as this introduction will hint, neither this country nor the wider world is heading towards an increasingly secularized society, then what sort of religious impulses will be dominant? Is it inevitable that the growth of *spirituality*, as characterized by the 'mind, body and spirit' sections of our high street bookshops, will continue unabated? What will be the fate of the 'New Age' movement? How can cathedrals respond to these shifts in a manner which is sensitive to people's questions, hopes and fears? How can they do so in a way which also remains faithful to the patterns and beliefs which lie central to the Christian faith?

Secular or not?

So vision, dreams and energy for reform, then, are only part of the picture. As Beeson hints, it is also the fast-changing background of contemporary culture which has caused cathedrals to respond or, perhaps, to be perceived in new ways. Seen positively, the explosion of tourism has made cathedrals into magnets for those modern pilgrims characterized so well by novelist David Lodge. These quasi-pilgrims have given up their missals for guidebooks, and take home trinkets and souvenirs in place of rosaries, crucifixes or scallop shells.[4]

Cathedrals are attracting increasing numbers of visitors, without their priests or lay custodians needing to make any invitation to bring them into these great buildings. But this same contemporary world has also presented acute challenges to the Church and to the Christian faith more broadly. Churchgoing has declined. This decline is chronicled by Beeson; it is a phenomenon adverted to daily in articles by journalists on radio, television and in national newspapers. We live, we are told, in a profoundly secularized world where religion has been driven to the margins, and where few are bothered by the claims of a transcendent God – or do we?

During the 1960s, both sociologists of religion and theologians spilt much ink in defining the characteristics and personality of a secularized world. Secularization was defined both functionally and theologically. Functionally, there was no denying that during the late nineteenth century, and throughout the twentieth century, activities and initiatives previously undertaken by the Church, sometimes over centuries, were rapidly becoming the responsibility of the State. Health care and education are two obvious examples, but with the creation of the welfare state by the post-Second World War Labour government, other aspects of social care, formerly pioneered by the Church, also became the responsibility of the State. The State advanced into areas previously seen to be the preserve of the churches.

Alongside this, secularization theory argued that, in the traditional sense, religious consciousness was being pushed to the margins of people's experience. Theologians and religious commentators responded to this new world. This led to a spate of books, the most famous of which is probably Harvey Cox's *The Secular City*.[5] Closely allied to this was the development of a secularized gospel which became known as *Death of God Theology*.[6] There was a flurry of books written to respond to this analysis – on prayer, theology and pastoral care. What would Christian discipleship look like in a secularized world?

There is no doubting the significance of the work done in the 1960s on secularization, but, 40 years later, new research and new empirical factors call for a reassessment. So, on the empirical or functional level, there has been a withdrawal of State intervention in a

3

variety of areas of social welfare;[7] the State cannot, or ought not to, intervene. Instead, partnership with the voluntary sector, including the churches, is now seen as the way forward. Furthermore, the churches have, once again, continued to pioneer new work in this area. Cicely Saunders's founding of hospice care is the most obvious example. These shifts begin to undermine a simple functionalist secularization theory. The churches are, ironically, beginning to take a more prominent part once again in these areas of national life. It is the State which is in retreat, rather than the churches.

There has also developed a very significant critique of secularization theory itself by leading sociologists of religion, including those who contributed to the establishment of that theory in the 1960s. One of the most cogent critiques is that set out by Grace Davie in a series of recent books.[8] The essence of her critique is most concisely argued in her Sarum Lectures for 2001.[9] In this critique, which she subtitles *Parameters of Faith in the Modern World*, Davie expounds an analysis which has common strands with the recent work of both Peter Berger and David Martin, two other distinguished sociologists working in this area. Her work also resonates with other writers reflecting upon the impact of religion in world politics.[10] 'Desecularization theory' draws its evidence from the influence and practice of religion across the board and not just in relation to Christianity.

Vicarious religion

Extending the thesis outlined in her earlier books, Davie contrasts religion in Europe with religion in other continents; she focuses on Christianity notably in Africa, Asia and Latin America. In each of these continents Christianity is vibrant and growing in a variety of different cultural contexts. Europe is thus the exception to the rule. Furthermore, she argues that European religion is now no longer a model for export as it was in the case of the earlier colonial period; it is Europe that is idiorhythmic and not the rest of the world. European countries are not less religious because they are more rational, but because they are less and less capable of maintaining the memory which lies at the heart of their religious existence. They are, she suggests, amnesiac societies. The question then is posed – how can modern European societies overcome such amnesia? Her earlier analysis, *Religion in Modern Europe*, shows how the churches also remain key players in the voluntary sector.

With regard to the focus of this book, however, perhaps the key point is that modern Europe has spawned a phenomenon that can only be described as 'vicarious religion'. So, to quote from Davie's summary:

> Could it be that Europeans are not so much less religious than populations in other parts of the world, but – quite simply – differently so? For particular historical reasons (notably the historic connections between Church and State), significant numbers of Europeans are content to let both churches and churchgoers enact a memory on their behalf (the essential meaning of vicarious), more than half aware that they might need to draw on the capital at crucial times in their individual or collective lives.[11]

Mission-shaped cathedrals?

This part of the analysis has a mixed message for cathedrals. If this extension to the 'believing-without-belonging' thesis can be sustained, then the anonymity of cathedrals would explain why, in so many cases, cathedral congregations are growing where parish church congregations are frequently declining. Cathedrals form a 'half-way house' in such a society. People can belong, but in a rather more 'arms-length' manner. Nonetheless, there is one further and contrasting element to the argument. If the reason for this different pattern of religious engagement (or even disengagement) relates to the particular history of Church and State in Europe, with the strong historical links between the two, then what might this say about the position of cathedrals? Cathedrals represent, in many ways, the historic Church–State links classically. They are often seen as ecclesiastical pillars of the establishment. Does this not argue for a distancing between the non-belonging believers and cathedrals? This leads us towards a discussion of how cathedrals fit into a wider ecclesiology, or set of ecclesiologies. What is the relationship of cathedrals to a wider theology of the Church?

This issue has been focused sharply by the statistics indicating a numerical decline in the strength of the parish church. Indeed, it has challenged the churches to investigate more fully other patterns of churchgoing and, to use the current unattractive shorthand, different ways of 'being church'. This analysis has tended to concentrate on new forms of *network church* which are believed to be rooted in the different patterns of life being adopted in contemporary society.[12] The argument is that geographical focuses are no longer necessarily the most appropriate way forward. This, however, easily ignores the fact that non-geographical patterns of churchgoing are no new phenomenon. There are numerous examples which are far from fresh expressions. The 'deaf church' is, for example, a form of network church rooted in the particular needs of certain individuals and, indeed, a diffuse community. The post-war enthusiasm for industrial chaplaincy, pioneered by Ted Wickham and others, suggested that work-based Christian communities were another model. Hospital and educational chaplaincy work provides further examples.

What, then, of cathedrals? Certainly, there is clear evidence for growth in the numbers attending cathedrals as members of regular worshipping congregations. This shift is all the more obvious if one compares the situation in the mid- to late nineteenth century with the pattern of cathedral attendance in the late twentieth century.[13] It would be facile to argue that this transformation is accounted for by one factor only. There has been a series of cathedral reforms from the nineteenth century onwards and, undoubtedly, this has helped to make cathedrals more attractive to regular worshippers. Further, the aesthetic, heritage and pilgrimage qualities of cathedrals have become much more evident in a society where tourism has become a paramount industry. This too increases the attractiveness of cathedrals, and draws people from the local communities, both to conserve and also to use cathedrals as their own centres for worship.

Cathedrals, belonging and theologies of the Church

Nonetheless, the move pinpointed by Grace Davie and others towards 'believing without belonging' makes cathedrals more attractive to those who feel an allegiance to the Christian faith, but who are wary of too much commitment. The maintenance of parish churches, in everything from worship to the fabric, requires a highly committed core of people who are prepared to invest more than just the hour or two demanded by weekly worship. Cathedrals allow for a far looser connection. Indeed, it is notoriously difficult to encourage committed giving; the assumption among many worshippers is that cathedrals are richly endowed and supported financially in other ways. This cuts both ways. For, ironically, there are good reasons for applying a subtlety when encouraging commitment by regular cathedral worshippers. The 'stakeholders' in cathedrals are many and various, from the local diocese, through numerous local voluntary groups to the city and county communities. Pressing regular cathedral congregations to too great a commitment may encourage them to see themselves as the sole stakeholders. This results in a proprietorial stance, which takes cathedrals towards the model that operates in parish churches. The legislation which followed the work of the Howe Commission was careful to avoid this pitfall.

This means that the characteristics of a cathedral ecclesiology will be a subtle and differing blend of the relationships that exist with the various stakeholders. By ecclesiology we mean precisely how we understand the theology of the Church. At the heart of a cathedral's *raison d'être* there is a direct relationship with the communion ecclesiology which has become one of the established theological models since the Second Vatican Council. It is an ecclesiology which will relate the cathedral to the worldwide Church through the bishop, inasmuch as the cathedral is the focus of the bishop's teaching role within the diocese. Alongside this, however, must be placed a series of other ecclesiological connections more closely related to a theology rooted in the kingdom of God and that kingdom's latent existence throughout the wider world. Such reflections will encompass, particularly, those aspects of a cathedral's ministry which relate to tourists, to the lonely, to the casualties of our society, and which prompt a prophetic concern for social and individual ethical issues. An appreciation of the kingdom that God is already establishing in the world will also encompass those elements of a cathedral's work which relate it to the city, the county and the multitude of secular organizations which see the cathedral as theirs too.

There is, then, a third aspect of cathedral ecclesiology which is drawn towards that nebulous, but increasingly popular, word *spirituality*. Spirituality is an elusive word within Christian theology, but more elusive still when the boundaries are set more widely. Here one might begin with those who would identify themselves self-consciously as Christian pilgrims. They come, we are told, to visit shrines. The perception of cathedrals as shrines or sacred space can be a double-edged sword.[14] Nonetheless, where the cathedral treats pilgrimage as a *liminal* experience, taking people over a threshold and returning them to their own homes challenged, but also fed by the gospel, then a healthy theology of place can be developed. When, however, the journey is seen as an end in itself with the cathedral taking on the identity of a numinous oasis in a contemporary spiritual desert, sacred *space* and *place* are less healthy labels. Spirituality is, moreover, now seen as an all-embracing term reaching well beyond the confines of orthodox Christian doctrine; 'New Age' and new religious movements are happy to use the term.

The role of cathedrals here will need to be sensitive, both welcoming the seeker but also offering an interpretation of their experience within the broad categories of the Christian life. A rediscovery of the medieval use of labyrinths has proved to be helpful here. As one author notes later in this book, both within and outside Grace Cathedral in San Francisco there is a copy of the ancient labyrinth at Chartres. In the cloister at Norwich there is also a replica of a traditional labyrinth. Labyrinths can begin with the generalized spiritual quest, and lead people into understanding more clearly the Christian life as a journey towards Christ.

Slicing the cathedral cake

These brief reflections on ecclesiology indicate the delicate theological tapestry which can weave together some very different strands, and which may have helped cathedrals to assume a more significant place in the contemporary Church. This shift might have something to say to the Church more broadly. The aim of this book is to gather together reflections on cathedrals from a wide variety of angles, to help understand why both the perceptions and uses of cathedrals have changed, but also to see how reflection on this can enrich not only our ecclesiology, but also our understanding of Christian mission in contemporary society. So, to slice through the experience and being of cathedrals at different angles, and from different directions, may offer new insights into Christian mission and its relationships with both theology and religious experience.

So the slices through the cake are various. What can the archaeologist tell us? Is the conservation lobby right in arguing against significant alteration to medieval fabric, or have cathedrals always evolved, and does the history of their developing fabric help us better to understand how these remarkable buildings have differently ministered to the wider community throughout history? If that is so, then perhaps we can appreciate, more profoundly, the stimulus that has led to *Les grands projets*, to pick up a French architectural metaphor. There has been an acceleration in cathedral development, and it would be interesting and informative to understand the deeper issues behind this.

Then, in a number of ways, cathedrals relate structurally more than they have in the recent past to other agencies within society. Through partnerships with local educational authorities far more children now enter cathedrals on a daily basis; this is seen as a key part of secular education, and as a part of cathedral outreach. At the other end of the educational system universities now partner cathedrals in a variety of innovative ways. So, what does this say about cathedrals as communities themselves, and about how they might now be seen in the wider community? Responses to this question may also be different from the more recently established cathedrals set within the context of highly populated urban communities.

Each of these questions will have an impact on how the Church sees its cathedrals and the role they believe they have in the Church; we have already alluded to the need to reflect on ecclesiology. But how does a broad or layered ecclesiology impinge upon the liturgy which is at the very heart of a cathedral's life. Cathedrals, after all, are the prime example of those places where the worship of God is offered daily, at least every morning and evening for all who may wish to attend – either caught up in the midst of the liturgy, or as those who stand on the edge gazing from a distance. They are also pre-eminently those churches which open themselves most frequently to institutions both sacred and secular, and offer the activities of these groups some liturgical expression. We should, of course, emphasize at this point that the chapters which follow deal uniquely with the cathedrals of the Church of England. There are also Roman Catholic cathedrals in England, and other great church buildings, which act effectively as cathedrals for churches within the Orthodox tradition. These great church buildings stand outside the scope of this book.

This introduction began with an extract from Trevor Beeson's recent book *The Deans*. That may also be a good place to end, as we engage with the process of slicing the cake in different directions. In his final chapter Beeson is more speculative, and describes how he sees the role of the cathedral dean in this new millennium. The dean is designated as *the missionary leader – looking ahead*. At one point, Beeson notes:

> Strong centres for [a] mission-orientated form of church life would be provided by a cathedral and, say, five other large churches in key geographical locations in the diocese. Each must enjoy the degree of independence necessary for a flexible response to changing circumstances in their areas.[15]

Beeson sees a seminal role for cathedrals in a fast-changing world. They may even share a broad and diverse role with other 'great churches'.

Beeson is clear that cathedrals must retain an independence from their dioceses and that they offer a unique ministry in contemporary society. Do the following pages support or undermine his thesis?

Notes

1 Trevor Beeson, *The Deans* (London, SCM Press, 2004), p. 1.
2 *Heritage and Renewal: The Report of the Archbishops' Commission on Cathedrals* (London, Church House Publishing, 1994).
3 Stephen Platten and Christopher Lewis (eds), *Flagships of the Spirit* (London, Darton, Longman and Todd, 1998).
4 David Lodge, *Paradise News* (Harmondsworth, Penguin Books, 1991). See especially pp. 75–6.
5 Harvey Cox, *The Secular City* (Harmondsworth, Penguin, 1968).

6 See, for example, Thomas Altizer, *The Gospel of Christian Atheism* (London, Collins, 1967); Paul von Buren, *The Secular Meaning of the Gospel Based on an Analysis of Its Language* (London, SCM Press, 1963).

7 Cf. Stephen Platten (ed.), *The Retreat of the State* (Norwich, Canterbury Press, 1999).

8 See, for example, Grace Davie, *Religion in Britain since 1975: Believing without Belonging* (Oxford, Blackwell, 1994), and *Religion in Modern Europe: A Memory Mutates* (Oxford, Oxford University Press, 2000).

9 Grace Davie, *Europe – the Exceptional Case* (London, Darton, Longman and Todd, 2002). See especially Chapters 1 and 6.

10 See, for example, John L. Esposito and Michael Watson (eds), *Religion and Global Order* (Cardiff, University of Wales Press, 2000).

11 Davie, *Europe – the Exceptional Case*, p. 19.

12 *Mission-shaped Church: Church Planting and Fresh Expressions of Church in a Changing Context* (London, Church House Publishing, 2004) (a Church of England report).

13 Cf., for example, Edward Meyrick Goulburn, *The Goulburn Norwich Diaries*, ed. Noel Henderson (Norwich, Canterbury Press, 1996), *passim*; and also Owen Chadwick, *The Victorian Church*, 2 vols (London, A. & C. Black, 1970), especially vol. 2, pp. 366–95.

14 Cf. John Inge, *A Christian Theology of Place* (London, Ashgate, 2003).

15 Beeson, *The Deans*, p. 237.

2

Masks and mission:
Cathedrals and their communities

GRAHAM JAMES

━━━━◆◆◆━━━━

In 1989 Danny Danziger published *The Cathedral.*[1] His book features interviews with 40 different people who 'had given their lives' to Lincoln Cathedral. Danziger had lived in the shadow of that great minster church for several months. It cast its spell on him. In each of the chapters (all quite short and dedicated to just one of these characters) you hear authentic voices. All seem to find a different vocabulary to describe their relationship with the cathedral. They see it and each other from contrasting perspectives, observing this great church and its life through the prism of their own experience. Hence the Lord Lieutenant speaks of the Queen's visit and great county occasions. An 88-year-old flower arranger talks less about her love of flowers and more about her long connection with the cathedral, relishing the past while fully enjoying the present. She hopes for a nice funeral and trusts that her ashes will eventually be interred in the cloisters. She belongs to this cathedral. It is hers. Then a verger speaks of sometimes finding a special corner to be alone in the great building, a way of having the cathedral to herself for a while. She says she has to visit the cathedral when she comes home from holiday as if to greet an old friend again. Even the job titles of some of those Danny Danziger interviews tell you a story. There's the Domus Supervisor, who turns out to be a cross between a locksmith and head of security. You come to realize that the cathedral is a complex place. There is clearly no such thing as a single cathedral community. There are many communities, some barely conscious of any others but each in a relationship with the building. Even those most closely associated with the worship – the lay clerks, for example – comment on the magnetism of the place while acutely aware of its physical limitations at choral evensong on a freezing February weekday.

These interviews capture mixed emotions. Affection is partnered frequently by irritation. Even the scale and domination of the great church on the hill can be forbidding. The most ambivalent interviews are those with the clergy. One speaks with great candour about the tensions and conflicts between the Dean and Chapter. The gravity of the differences is serious and ongoing. There's even an interview with the incoming Dean, which strikes the reader who knows of the even more serious and far-reaching conflicts to follow as uncannily prescient.[2] What is striking, however, about the majority of the interviews with the lay people who work in a paid or voluntary capacity in and around the cathedral is that they rarely mention the clergy at all. These clerical differences either pass them by or make no impact on their lives. Perhaps that's because there's something very direct in the relationship between them and their cathedral. It doesn't need clerical mediators. There's a surprisingly personal character in the relationship between this massive building and the great variety of people who inhabit it and surround it. Perhaps they represent the wider community's appreciation of the cathedral more accurately than the clergy, even if the latter can talk about such things more easily.

Were the conflicts and tensions revealed by Danziger's interviews peculiar to Lincoln? After all, this was a tinderbox waiting to explode. Yet I'm sure Danny Danziger could have gone to almost any of our ancient cathedrals, and to many of our more modern ones as well, and produced a similar set of interviews. He would have found people living in an intense relationship with a great religious building, and many of those people might not count themselves religious at all. Perhaps Danziger could have gone on to interview those at further remove, for cathedrals are iconic buildings for many who rarely enter them. As it is, there are many communities competing for space in any cathedral. For each of them it is 'our' cathedral. The instinct of the verger to find her 'space' is one of deep affection but also potentially proprietorial. Cathedrals have many proprietors. The dean and chapter are but one. Even so, it often falls to them to negotiate the ways communities within and well beyond the cathedral do not simply feel welcome but come to recognize a rightful place in its economy, a place that can never be exclusive. But how is it that a building that is so awesome, constructed on a greater than human scale ('to bring us soonest to our knees' as J. L. Pearson said of Truro) can inspire intimacy? How can a cathedral become so personal? What are we to make of such a personal relationship?

The cathedral as 'person'

The word 'person' comes from the Latin *persona*, meaning *mask*. A mask was often worn by an actor in the theatre. It was the means of taking on a particular character. Nowadays we refer to persons in all sorts of different ways. Sometimes we simply mean individual human beings, but at other times we refer to something being 'on your person' as being deeply connected with the body and its clothing. Being 'in person' means being physically present. The law has long recognized the 'corporate person'. In his book *England: An Elegy*,[3] written at the turn of the millennium, Roger Scruton explored the significance of 'the corporate person'.

> The law recognises the 'corporate person', such as the firm, the church or the university, which can take decisions, assume responsibility, pursue goals and acquire rights and duties in the world of negotiation to which you and I belong. This legal construct gives judicial recognition to a social fact. Every form of human membership casts a personal shadow which marches behind us or in front of us, above us or below, and which takes on a moral reality of its own. It is the product of our decisions. It also gradually transcends them, becoming an object of loyalty, affection or resentment, just like you and me. Such 'artificial persons' are also in a sense natural, since it is in our nature to create them, to acknowledge them, and to relate to them in the way in which we relate to each other.[4]

Roger Scruton warms to his theme in relation to the monarchy and to England herself. Nowhere does he mention cathedrals in this connection but much of what he has to say applies readily to them, and is well illustrated in Danny Danzinger's interviews. But, to use Scruton's metaphor, what sort of shadow does the cathedral as a 'corporate person' cast over the communities, the city and the county which surround it? The shadow of the human person lengthens as the sun sets in the sky. Does the shadow of the corporate person of an English cathedral embrace a wider community more easily since the bright blaze of the Christian religion has faded in England? If so, it would be a curious development that these buildings, so expressive of a confident faith, should turn out to be of such utility in an age of religious uncertainty. Are cathedrals particularly effective when the religious identity, even the corporate personality, of England is weak? Have they the power to wear a mask that we long to recognize, and with which we identify, but which is more difficult to locate in an atomized and secular society? The encouraging vibrancy of cathedrals in relation to their surrounding communities should prompt us to ask whether this is particularly facilitated in England by the looseness of our hold upon our religious identity, enabling us to give the cathedral a mask, a personality in a bewildering variety of images.

The cathedral wearing the mask of blessing

In October 2003 the University of East Anglia (UEA) held a service in Norwich Cathedral to mark the fortieth anniversary of the university's foundation. We have now become accustomed to celebrating almost any anniversary, however insignificant, in both secular and religious life. Cathedrals have made a small industry of our need to validate the uncertainties of the present by commemorating the securities of the past. In *The Deans*[5] Trevor Beeson notes that the 800th anniversary of Westminster Abbey in 1865 was marked by a single service. In 1965 the 900th anniversary was observed by a full year of events. The pace has quickened even since then.

Prior to the service in Norwich Cathedral, the new Chancellor of the University of East Anglia, Sir Brandon Gough, was installed in his office at a ceremony which took place before the nave altar. The first physical manifestation of the university had been an office in the Cathedral Close so the connection was unforced.

The whole event may have seemed fairly unremarkable to most observers. One of the Norwich clergy brought his video camera to the cathedral that afternoon simply to record whatever was happening. He had no idea that this big university occasion was taking place. The policy of allowing the general public to move around the cathedral (including side aisles) during services meant that his eventual 15-minute film records both the academic procession (rather outdoing the Bishop's procession for colour and drama since the academic dress at the UEA was designed by Cecil Beaton) as well as visitors of all shapes and sizes doing their own thing, largely oblivious to the surrounding drama. For them, people dressing up for big ceremonies was the sort of thing cathedrals did. Here was cathedral and university in full establishment fig. It may have seemed a bit old fashioned, the sort of tradition likely to fade away, but its survival even in 2003 may have surprised few.

Yet all this was more surprising and novel than even some of those who were taking part may have recognized. When the University of East Anglia marked its twenty-fifth anniversary there was no service in the cathedral even though the vice-chancellor of the time, a loyal Anglican, would have liked one. There was a secular celebration elsewhere in the city instead. So what had changed? The increased contact between cathedral and university in the intervening years must not be minimized. But it is doubtful that the change was due simply to different personalities or even the consequence of some of the collaborative initiatives of the past decade.[6]

What was the mask that the cathedral wore for the university that day? In other words, why was Norwich Cathedral of such utility to a modern, secular university? The university staff and students have not become more religious in the past 40 years but somehow a cathedral service now seems a more natural way of expressing thanksgiving and seeking a blessing than it may have done a generation ago. The university was then the new kid on the block, looking confidently to the future, perhaps expecting to sweep all before it. Although much had been done in the late 1950s and early 1960s by civic and county leadership (including that of the Bishop of Norwich at the time) to bring a university to Norwich, the early years of its history were not noted for harmonious and creative relationships between the university and the city. Perhaps there was impatience, expressed partly through student unrest with established institutions, whereas in more recent years all institutions have sensed their need of each other and a shared common cultural purpose. Perhaps also the fortieth anniversary service was an illustration that it does not take long for something as new as the University of East Anglia to become part of the established order in England. It is intriguing that the UEA should have published a 500-page hardback book on its history while just 40 years old.[7] Its sense of itself has altered. It does now have a history. It may not be as lengthy as the cathedral's, but its place in the life of city and county is hugely significant. When an institution comes to reflect on its history it does want to give thanks. It seeks to find its place in relation to the wider community in which it is set, a community for which the cathedral is iconic. (Norwich Union would not have utilized the cathedral spire for its logos over so many years if that was not the case.) In uncertain times for universities, perhaps it's understandable that they look to cathedrals for the blessings that come from association with their stability and continuity. The assurance that 'all will be well, and all manner of things will be well', to borrow the phrase of a resident of Norwich some centuries ago,[8] is commonly sought by a huge variety of organizations and institutions which come for their thanksgiving and anniversary services (as well as their own carol services) to cathedrals up and down the land. The cathedral wears its mask of blessing in an unforced way. It comes naturally to it. Even if this is not an age seeking God it is certainly one seeking blessings. Where else wears that mask so well?

The cathedral wearing the mask of inclusion

The short amateur film recorded by the Norwich priest on the day when the university came to the cathedral in solemn state has many images. Children playing in the cloisters; mothers chatting to each other; a couple eating sandwiches; visitors pushing prams; vergers rearranging chairs; people lighting candles, kneeling quietly; others simply gazing into space; one or two engaged in animated discussion with a guide; others curious about what was taking place in the nave; still others walking past the event down a side aisle seemingly oblivious to it. Why were they there? Vergers and guides apart, everyone else had made a decision to come to the cathedral, whether planned or spontaneous, that Saturday afternoon. They did not make a community in themselves, but the cathedral was large enough to include them without asking them any questions or seeking from them any justification for being there. While the cathedral church is defined in relation to the *cathedra*, the seat of the bishop, it is unmistakable that the scale of the building does have a significant impact upon the character of its ministry. A parish church can generally only do one thing at a time whereas an ancient cathedral like Norwich can host a service with a large congregation and yet be used in all sorts of other ways while it is happening. The aspirations of English parish church cathedrals are generally entirely in conformity with those of the more ancient foundations, and yet the loss of scale or of a visual impact upon the skyline does create limitations. Spaciousness in a cathedral does have a liberating quality in our present age. What was once regarded as likely to be forbidding is now a vehicle for 'letting be'.

'Welcome to your Cathedral' is the common greeting of deans and canons across England to congregations at special services or on diocesan occasions. The message is clear. The cathedral should be somewhere where all can find their place. This has been expressed up and down the country by such initiatives as The Big Draw, Find Out Fairs (where cathedrals are used as places where people may come for information about access to adult education, careers and voluntary organizations), history days, family fun days and a host of other initiatives to draw people into our cathedrals who may not otherwise think they are places for them. The hosting of television programmes like *Antiques Roadshow* in a cathedral nave, as at Truro, or editions of *Mastermind* as well as various *Raves in the Nave* (as they were known a decade or more ago) all illustrate attempts to broaden even further a cathedral's appeal. Something as simple and straightforward as clearing the nave of chairs, as at York Minster or at Liverpool, has enabled these great spaces to speak of a freedom that a parish church clothed in fixed wooden pews can never emulate. And at York a festival has developed and grown, almost spontaneously, as a result of the clearance of the nave.

A young woman, probably not yet 21 years of age, approached a verger in one of our cathedrals, asking if she could see a priest. It was just before 8.30 a.m. He got the priest who had just celebrated the 8.00 a.m. Eucharist to speak with the woman. She had two children, one aged almost three and the other a few months old, and they had both been taken into care. She was living separately from her partner and her life was in a mess. She was waiting to know whether she might get her children back. The priest prayed with her and blessed her. She said, 'I love coming here. I don't know what it is but it feels different. It feels as if I belong here.'

That young woman came to the cathedral because she found the early morning the worst time to be without her children. She would be getting them up, dressing them, preparing breakfast. It was when she felt most alone. She was entirely unchurched, and yet came to a cathedral, walking past a good many parish churches to do so. Why did she think the cathedral was for her in a way parish churches were not?

Is it the case that parish churches, and churches of other traditions as well, seem to be dominated and owned by their congregations in a way cathedrals are not? Is that one of the reasons why cathedrals are seen, by contrast, as for everyone? A cathedral can be a spiritual home for those with little faith or even no faith at all. (It is intriguing how many atheists and agnostics love choral evensong.) Cathedrals have become centres of interfaith activity in cities where such a ministry has been needed. Even where this is not so, the Anne Frank Exhibition has found a natural home in these locations. Jews have also found cathedrals a welcoming setting for events surrounding Holocaust Memorial Day.

The cathedral, itself a community of communities, becomes the home, temporarily, of many other communities, somewhere many may feel they belong. This is a powerful witness to social harmony and a telling testimony to the Christian belief that all people are made in the image and likeness of God himself. But are there limits to this inclusion? Is it made feasible only by a diminished sense of Christian distinctiveness? Are those who criticize cathedrals as the bastion of an outdated sixties liberalism right?

While clergy may offer a welcome to 'your cathedral' to all and sundry, anyone responding to such a welcome by seeking to be married or to have a family funeral in 'their' cathedral may discover that it is not quite theirs as much as they have been led to believe. They will find themselves redirected to their parish church. 'Your cathedral' only has meaning if there is a bishop with the care of all the churches and whose focus in mission and ministry is where his teaching seat is found.

Removing the mask of inclusion: tensions exposed

A recent visit to St Andrew's Cathedral in Sydney illustrated for me how a cathedral could let the mask of inclusion slip, or even seek to remove it completely. It also showed how much effort needs to be employed if a cathedral is to be a natural home for people of little faith or none. There is clearly something about a cathedral church, even in a country with no established religion (though Anglican cathedrals in Australia are built in the English tradition) which breathes an unconditional welcome, allowing people to use its sacred space as they wish. This may conflict with the prevailing theology of the clergy in charge, if they want it to wear only the mask of gospel challenge.

A good deal has been written about Sydney Anglicanism in its latest manifestation though I doubt whether casual visitors to St Andrew's Cathedral would pick up much unless they are especially keen eyed. It is certainly the case that the Lord's table is no longer a focus of the sanctuary but is now to be found unadorned in a side aisle and only moved to the chancel step when the Lord's Supper is celebrated. In its place before the reredos at the east end is a glass case with an open Bible, which, somewhat strangely, is locked, suggesting the Bible needs protection. It certainly needs an interpreter. The Sunday evening service is called *The Bible Talks*, though it is doubtful that it ever does so unaided. The pew leaflet of 27 February 2005 included an article by the Dean, focusing on the hymn by William Cowper 'Jesus, where'er thy people meet'. The Dean makes the point that 'it is wonderful to be reminded that God can be prayed to everywhere and anywhere and inhabits not a building but the humble mind'. The rest of the literature in the cathedral refers not to services or acts of worship but to 'Christians gathering'. A leaflet explains that

> St Andrew's Cathedral exists to help people come to know God and to grow in the faith, to build up the body of believers through mutual service of the gifts that God has given us, and to be involved in the proclamation of the saving news of Jesus.

Who could argue with that? Yet it is incomplete as an expression of the particular vocation of a cathedral church. It fails to recognize that the distinctive character of a cathedral church lies in its connection with the ministry and mission of the bishop, whose *cathedra* makes this church what it is. 'The seat of the bishop and a centre for worship and mission' is how the Cathedrals Measure 1999, Section 1 defined it.

Among the English public, especially the non-churchgoing public, the cathedral is the bishop's church. Diocesan bishops will testify to the frequency with which they receive letters of complaint (and, thankfully, occasional praise) about the cathedrals of which they are assumed to be in charge. People may have little idea about what a bishop does but they do have an instinctive sense that he is for everyone. His very title – the Bishop of London, the Bishop of Coventry, the Bishop of Norwich – does not suggest a limited ecclesiastical role but a ministry of representation, advocacy and pastoral care for all people in a particular place. (Deans are also denoted in the same way, yet the solecism 'the Dean of x Cathedral' is becoming increasingly common – perhaps a significant social shift.)

How individual bishops relate to their cathedrals may vary as much as the extent to which they use them as an integral part of their own mission. Even so, every cathedral has a constant symbolic reminder of this wider ministry in the *cathedra*. No cathedral can escape its sense of connection with the wider diocese. The very rationale of the cathedral expands its own sense of mission and connectedness with communities at some distance from it. A cathedral is called to be the mother church of other churches. It is beckoned by its very character to look outwards and become immersed in the wider world beyond its doors, just as any bishop should. This is what makes a cathedral what it is, whatever its size. This is also what makes cathedrals different to parish churches. A parish church, even when built on a cathedral scale, cannot achieve fully the range and influence of a cathedral's ministry. Spaciousness may be on the side of a great building like Selby Abbey or a huge parish church like St Nicholas, Great Yarmouth, and that spaciousness may be used creatively to include all sorts and conditions in its life. But it remains a parish church with a mission focused on the geographical community it is called to serve. That is its purpose, and it is different.

St Andrew's Cathedral in Sydney seemed to draw little, if any, attention to its role as the seat of a bishop. Yet the memorials on the walls represented a heritage that was undeniably episcopal. St Andrew's is clearly more than a simple preaching room but its inherent, implicit and inclusive mask was one that seemed to be kept in check, if not hidden. The natural theology of a cathedral church, if one can speak of such a thing, seemed to be in tension with the emphatic concentration on a biblical preaching ministry alone.

A cathedral is a place where Christians gather but its mission, like that of the bishop himself, is not limited to this congregational dimension of church life. The cathedral certainly finds its identity in its daily worship, its proclamation of the saving work of God in Christ, and the rhythms of the Church's year helping it to live out the story of salvation in its daily life.[9] These are some of the things which give the cathedral its special character. It isn't simply a great empty space for people to invest with a meaning of their own, a divine version of the National Exhibition Centre at Birmingham or Earls Court in London. In themselves, these buildings are empty of meaning. The cathedral, by contrast, is full of its own understanding of why God made the world and how he has redeemed its fallen nature. It is the cathedral's confidence in the Christian faith that makes it spacious and inclusive, just as the teaching of Jesus made him easy to approach for the stranger, the person in need, the community that felt marginalized, whether it was the boy with the loaves and fishes, the woman with the haemorrhage or the Samaritan woman at the well, to take just three examples. The cathedral lets them, like Jesus, find their own way after the encounter. There is less pressure in a cathedral upon those who enter it to gather with other Christians. The cathedral's witness is not only found in the preached word or the open Bible. It has a history, tradition and symbolism which means that it is more than an empty space or humble room for preaching.

The cathedral wearing the mask of place of prayer

Any church is a place of prayer. English cathedrals are prayed in more than they were a generation ago. Special places are set aside for prayer. But not at Sydney. I imagine it is the linking of prayer with particular locations within the cathedral church (let alone through votive candles as visual aids to prayer) that would not be part of the Sydney tradition. Nor were they part of the tradition of most English cathedrals two or three generations ago. Things have changed radically. Anglican cathedrals in England now have as many candles lit in them on a daily basis by those offering prayer as their Roman Catholic counterparts, perhaps more. The cathedrals of the Church of England have become again places where people come to pray. Cathedral authorities have responded to demand. People have put the prayer mask firmly back on our cathedrals. It's a mask cathedrals wear very comfortably.

A couple of mornings after the tragic events of September 11th, 2001, in New York the local BBC TV News crew came to Norwich Cathedral simply to film the area that had been set up for people to write in a book of condolence, to pray and to light candles. A number of people were already queuing to sign. One woman signed the book, offered a prayer and lit a candle, and when interviewed for television said to camera, 'I'm on my way to work. I'm not religious but I had to come.'

The instinct and desire to pray does not seem to have ebbed as significantly as the 'long withdrawing roar' of the sea of faith. Matthew Arnold, in his famous poem,[10] pictures human beings 'on a darkling plain, Swept with confused alarm of struggle and flight . . .' It is this experience, perhaps even more intense when the sea of faith has withdrawn, which still inspires the instinct to pray.

Cathedrals provide the place for communities and individuals to pray in an age which has not lost the instinct to pray but scarcely knows how to do it. A young man queuing in a cathedral following the death of Diana, Princess of Wales, signed the condolence book and then asked a steward if there was anywhere he could pray. 'Wherever you like' came the answer. Later the young man approached the steward again for help in how to pray.

Our cathedrals are more geared to providing the place to pray than the instruction. This may be an area where more needs to be done. Ours is a society that needs schools of prayer. Many are ready to be instructed in meditation, and may grow through prayer to faith in the God to whom we pray. They do not frequently look to the churches for help in this area, but cathedrals are astonishingly well placed to take a lead in recovering the practice of prayer for the Christian tradition. Perhaps our cathedrals should employ directors of prayer or tutors in spirituality as often as they employ visitor officers or education teams. The wider community now seems to associate cathedrals with prayer more easily than parish churches. Our cathedrals do not seem to be responding as imaginatively as they might to the new opportunities this creates. Communities need holy places, validated by prayer. Cathedrals provide them.

Our cathedrals wearing these masks of blessing, inclusion and as places of prayer are not really taking on different personalities, but revealing different modes of one being. What each of them has in common is a willingness to be used as a place of spiritual discovery. The cathedral does not have to wear its mask of Christian commitment heavily since its daily life and worship are a constant reminder of its character and identity. So too in its role as the place where priests and deacons are ordained, where the bishop confirms, where the mission of the diocese finds focus and renewal, the cathedral finds its rationale. Those who make up the communities within the cathedral itself, those with whom I started, use the cathedral for their own purposes just as much as those at some special service, or tourists and pilgrims or those who, even though they are not religious, simply call in to pray. The cathedral church is at the service of the wider community since it is willing to be used, and many are willing to use it. Even so we should not neglect to recognize the significant proportion of any population surrounding cathedrals who have never entered their doors, especially among those under 40 years of age. But many do come – in groups, with organizations, in school parties, as individuals. In an age in which our parish churches and churches of other denominations become more distinctive as places of committed Christian faith, cathedrals may be easier to enter. They are certainly easier places in which to pray and worship for the uncommitted and the searching. It is the practice of prayer and worship that leads to belief and commitment, not the other way round. Too often we imagine that prayer and worship are the consequence of belief, not the means by which we find that we believe. Perhaps cathedrals have no new vocation in an age of unbelief, but have rediscovered the dynamics which, if only we understood them, might lead to another age of faith. They wear the mask of mission, after all.

Notes

1 Danny Danziger, *The Cathedral* (London, Viking, 1989).
2 A bitter dispute focused on the Dean and Sub-Dean was slow to resolve, despite the intervention of the Bishop and the Archbishop of Canterbury. A consistory court where the Dean was charged and cleared of an offence unrelated to the main dispute added to the difficulties.
3 Roger Scruton, *England: An Elegy* (London, Chatto & Windus, 2000).
4 Scruton, *England*, p. 70.
5 Trevor Beeson, *The Deans* (London, SCM Press, 2004), p. 57.
6 There have been various collaborative ventures between the UEA and Norwich Cathedral in the past decade. The annual Fleming lectures, Norwich Cathedral Institute and the siting of the Sainsbury Institute for Japanese Studies in the Cathedral Close are three examples.
7 Michael Sanderson, *The History of the University of East Anglia, Norwich* (London, Hambledon and London, 2002).
8 Referring to Julian of Norwich in her *Revelations of Divine Love*. A modern sculpture of Julian was dedicated in 2001, alongside one of St Benedict, filling niches in the west front of Norwich Cathedral.
9 The Church's year seems to be interpreted somewhat loosely at St Andrew's Cathedral, Sydney. The main Sunday morning service on Palm Sunday 2005 had the title 'Festival of Hymns for Easter'.
10 Matthew Arnold, 'Dover Beach'.

3

Cathedrals, outreach and education

JOHN INGE

Now what I want is, Facts. Teach these boys and girls nothing but facts. Facts alone are wanted in life. Plant nothing else, and root out everything else. You can only form the minds of reasoning animals upon Facts: nothing else will ever be of any service to them. This is the principle on which I bring up my own children, and this is the principle on which I bring up these children. Stick to Facts, sir.[1]

The philistine Mr Gradgrind, whom Charles Dickens introduces at the beginning of *Hard Times*, has often been used as the epitome of oppressive education but debate concerning the extent to which education should be about the imparting of facts has continued since Dickens's day. In our own era, learning facts by rote received a bad name in the liberal sixties and seventies but more recently the pendulum has swung in the other direction with the introduction of literacy and numeracy hours in primary schools. Behind such fashions and debates in education lies the basic question of what education is supposed to be about and for. Mr Gradgrind talks of forming the minds of young people and this would certainly need to include teaching them to read and write – though maybe not using Mr Gradgrind's methods. There is more to education, however, than the imparting of such basic 'life skills' and it is here that cathedrals can come into their own. Few facts associated with cathedrals are of any great significance: what does it matter, for example, that the central tower of Ely Cathedral fell on 12 February 1322? I have observed countless visitors being told this fact and am quite confident that every one of them will promptly have forgotten it. There can be no good reason for remembering it, anyway: it comes into the same category as the facts that there are 1,760 yards in a mile and 4,840 square yards in an acre, both of which I was made to learn at school and which have never been of any use to me since, except in pointing out the uselessness of such facts. There are great truths for which cathedrals stand, the truths of the Christian gospel, but truth is a much richer conception than fact. In an era which tends to view education in baldly utilitarian terms, cathedrals are well placed to witness that education is a richer, deeper and much more subtle affair than is often recognized.

Many of our ancient cathedrals were monastic institutions which, in the Middle Ages, were one of the few educational resources in their area. Later, cathedral schools were a vital part of the developing educational provision in this country. What of today, however? Though some cathedrals still have schools associated with them, cathedrals today have no formal or statutory educational role and are surrounded by myriad educational institutions well placed (and well funded) to provide education – factual and otherwise – for people of all ages. In these circumstances the vast educational potential of cathedrals is associated with their architectural, historical and social significance, with their aesthetic and artistic merit and, most importantly, with the way in which they are the home to living Christian communities. These things combine to make the cathedral a *sursum corda* (as it were, a lifting of the heart) in stone. That is to say, cathedrals can and should lift the heart above the everyday and towards God.

While I was ministering at Ely Cathedral we were fortunate to be able to organize a Pilgrim Train in conjunction with a local railway operating company. Having been deposited on the platform at Ely station, an entire trainful of 400 schoolchildren from Harlow in Essex walked the half-mile up the hill to the cathedral. They were met on their way by vergers and clergy, fully robed, and entered the cathedral in procession by its south door. The intention was that, after entering, the procession should turn east and make its way towards the site of the shrine of St Etheldreda, on which they would place bunches of flowers. They had received much preparation for this, not only learning about St Etheldreda and her foundation but also being told exactly what they should do upon entering the cathedral. Burns would have us believe that 'the best-laid schemes o' mice an' men gang aft agley' and that was certainly true in this case. Once the children had

entered the cathedral to the sound of the organ playing at full volume
and their eyes had wandered upwards to behold the staggering beauty
of the Octagon, they were completely overcome and the cathedral
stewards found it impossible to move them on. The whole procession
ground to a halt and it took the best part of half an hour to complete
the simple manoeuvre which had been planned.

Those children learned precious few facts while at the cathedral
but they underwent what will have been, if the anecdotal evidence
offered by adults who visited cathedrals as children and to whom I
have talked is anything to go by, one of the most memorable experiences of their childhood. What had the cathedral done for them? It
had acted as a *sursum corda* in stone. It had lifted up their hearts
and filled them with a sense of awe; it had reminded them, at a deep
level, that learning to be human is about more than learning facts and
figures. One of the reasons why I relished ministering in a cathedral
was the enormous potential that I felt cathedrals had for the gospel
and for the human flourishing which the gospel can and should
enable. What cathedrals can do is lift the heart and widen the hori-
zons of those who for most of their lives are subjected to a dull diet
of reductionist reasoning. It can awaken them to the importance of
spirituality.

There is much talk of spirituality in educational circles at present
but the sort I have in mind here is a full-blooded Christian one.
Donald Allchin eloquently evokes how this sort of spirituality might
relate to a cathedral:

> To speak of spirituality is to speak of that meeting of eternity with
> time, of heaven with earth; it is to recover a sense of the holiness of
> matter, the sacredness of this world of space and time when it is known
> as the place of God's epiphany . . . There is a geography of holy places,
> the places where the saints have dwelt . . . places whose beauty has
> been revealed by lives which have been open to God in such a way as
> to show that this world is not a system closed upon itself.[2]

What cathedrals can do – and did for those children – is to enable
a sense of awe, and a sense of awe is very close to worship. Albert
Einstein wrote: 'Whoever is devoid of wonder, whoever remains

unmoved, whoever cannot contemplate or know the deep shudder of the soul in enchantment, might just as well be dead for he has closed his eyes upon life.'[3] I have seen the same reaction engendered on many occasions when allowing adults to experience the cathedral in the evening when it is closed to the public. Such visits happen regularly but did so in a concentrated form in the Diocese of Ely when we decided to encourage people to make 1999 a year of preparation for the Millennium, a year of 'spiritual stocktaking'. All parishes received an invitation to come on an evening pilgrimage to the cathedral and a large proportion accepted. It was suggested that those who came should bring with them friends on the edges of the Church, and many did. My experience of leading them in pilgrimage reinforced my belief that helping people to feel a sense of awe is a very powerful evangelistic tool and, in our own time, perhaps the most valuable. Christians have expended much energy in the past talking about the 'facts' of sin and judgement when trying to interest people in God. Today, however, we live in a culture characterized by what Alistair McFadyen terms 'pragmatic atheism' in which many are bemused by any talk of sin – except, perhaps, in the context of eating chocolate. This is because 'we live in a culture which is basically secular, which affirms the world's integrity and independence from any external, non-worldly reality so that it may be understood in its own terms, without immediate or explicit reference to God'.[4] The commentator Brian Walden recently suggested that 'we ought to talk to each other more about the central mystery of life' and cathedrals can provide what has been referred to as 'open-minded space' to help people reflect on that mystery. In doing so they can restore a 'geography of holy places', to use Allchin's phraseology, to indicate that this world is not a system closed upon itself. They do this by speaking to people on many levels – not just the rational.

All this is a hugely important part of the Church's task. The novelist Susan Howatch tells of how she needed to 'hang around behind the pillars' of Westminster Abbey for some considerable time before she was ready to embrace the Christian faith. Conversion is increasingly being seen as process rather than event, a notion helpfully explored by Mike Booker and Mark Ireland in their book *Evangelism – Which Way*

Now? They remark that even the dramatic conversion stories re-counted in the Acts of the Apostles may best be understood in terms of a journey towards faith, and this is equally true of other conversion experiences in the New Testament: 'Peter's journey to faith occupies the whole of the period of Jesus' ministry, and if there is a conversion moment it cannot be definitely identified'.[5] Cathedrals can help people on their journey in life and faith. This was certainly the intention of those who built the great medieval cathedrals to be the destination of pilgrimage: the notion of journey was integral to their creation from the beginning. Not only were they intended to be the destination of pilgrimage but the pilgrimage continued within them upon entrance: pilgrims were guided through the building on a clear journey once they had arrived. The genius of pilgrimage is that it combines the power of a place associated with divine disclosure with the dynamic of movement, of journey, which is so helpful, symbolically, to Christian formation and life.

As has always been the case on pilgrimage, visitors to cathedrals should be helped to engage with them in a manner which enables connections to be made between the pilgrims' lives and the Christian gospel. A conscious attempt to do this was embarked upon at Ely when the Friends of the Cathedral made a generous donation for a work of art to commemorate the Millennium. Working with 'Theology through the Arts', a project of the Divinity Faculty at Cambridge University, we commissioned a huge piece in cast aluminium by Jonathan Clarke entitled *The Way of Life*. It is an enormous cross at the end of a winding path on the wall which people see, on their right, as they enter the cathedral by the great west door. The beauty of the chosen design is its simplicity: it articulates the theme of pilgrimage at the entrance of this great house of pilgrimage and relates the journey of life to the Cross, suggesting that life has meaning in so far as it is connected to the Cross. The design fulfils what could be argued to be the most important criteria to be applied to an artistic commission for a cathedral or church: it is aesthetically pleasing (both in itself and in the position for which it has been designed) *and* it has clear theological symbolism. Anecdotal evidence would suggest that it speaks eloquently to visitors and regular worshippers alike and that it has an important educational function. It does so, I would suggest, because it is a good example of what cathedrals should be doing for those who visit them, and what those who minister in cathedrals should be seeking to allow: the making of connections between the building, the life experiences of those who visit, and the Christian faith. Only in so far as people are able, at one level or another, to engage with this trinity will the cathedral have done what it is capable of doing for them educationally. This is not overt evangelism but it is deeply connected with the Christian gospel.

Reflection can also be assisted by exhibitions of various sorts. For example, an imaginative initiative entitled 'Labyrinth', which has toured cathedrals in the recent past, gives people space and quiet and makes use of the symbolism of the labyrinth, beloved of medievals and built into the fabric of some cathedrals. The finest surviving medieval labyrinth is at Chartres, of which there is an inside ('carpet copy') and an outside version at Grace Cathedral, San Francisco. In this modern version, people are invited to walk the labyrinth, assisted by various symbols and interactive media, and reflect. The most important part of the exercise, as with the evening pilgrimages at Ely Cathedral of which I made mention above, is to give people space both literal and metaphorical, to pose some searching questions and to enable them to reflect upon the central mystery of life.

It is sometimes said, rightly in my view, that cathedrals are the success story of the Church of England in the latter part of the twentieth century. There has been a remarkable blossoming in all sorts of areas, many of which are connected with education in one way or another, including the commissioning of works of art and the staging of exhibitions. They attract much larger congregations than they did 20 or 30 years ago and this, I think, is because of the sense of the transcendent which is present in cathedral worship at its best. During worship people are educated by readings and sermons, but cathedral worship – as all worship should – feeds the whole person at a much deeper level than words on their own can allow. Architecture and music combine to provide a feast for the senses – and it should be noted that cathedral music has not only survived, against the financial odds, but also has improved during this period. It is one of the great treasures not only of the Church of England but also of the English nation, and does much to educate in the broadest sense. In addition, most cathedrals play host to a considerable number of concerts and dramatic productions, all of which, if not specifically 'Christian', are in sympathy with the Christian faith. All this commendable activity does give rise to problems: several cathedrals have had to be proactive in introducing 'quiet hours' in order to restore the calm of the place and ensure that quiet reflection is possible at some times of day at least.

One sphere where this burgeoning of activity has been greatest is in the development of schools work. This is an area upon which cathedral authorities, knowing that many children never enter a church during their early years, have concentrated very hard. A majority of cathedrals now employs at least one qualified teacher as an education officer and they have done a remarkable job in recruiting and training volunteers who, together with the officers, welcome many thousands of schoolchildren each year to cathedrals. Education centres have been established in or adjacent to a number of cathedrals. They provide a space in which children can be welcomed and offered hospitality, as well as providing an area for engaging in 'hands-on' activities, so as to glean as much about the cathedral (and the faith for which it stands) as possible. The programme offered is normally very professional and, in addition to events for individual schools groups, many cathedrals organize imaginative 'schools days', such as those at Ely, for example, which attract nearly 4,000 children to the cathedral on four days in October.

The National Curriculum and agreed syllabi for religious education have been a great help in providing an incentive for schools to visit cathedrals: schools respond to the invitation to visit cathedrals with enthusiasm. However, this success carries with it dangers as well as opportunities. It is a matter of celebration that cathedrals have been able to show how they are relevant to many aspects of the National Curriculum – from science to history, from religious studies to mathematics – but one could be forgiven for thinking that the education departments of some cathedrals understand their task to be simply the delivery of the National Curriculum. The latter ensures that basic life skills are taught, but cathedrals should be about doing what it cannot do – enabling reflection on the significance and meaning of life itself. Sometimes this latter aim is not met by the wholly experiential approach adopted by some cathedrals. For example, children are often dressed up to experience the life of a medieval monk for a day and this can be hugely enjoyable but it will not be doing a great deal for those who are involved unless it enables them to make connections between the life that the monks lived and the meaning of their own lives. Why did monastics consecrate themselves in this manner and what is that saying to us today? The highly professional and imaginative manner in which cathedrals have risen to the challenge of encouraging schools to visit should be applauded, but those associated with cathedral education need to remember that unless everything they do helps people to engage with God they will have failed.

The schools work of cathedrals is something of which they can be justly proud. The picture with regard to adult education, however, is patchier. We live in an age when the Government, commendably, has placed much emphasis on 'lifelong learning' and many educational institutions have expanded their provision for people of all ages very greatly. Though there are imaginative things happening, it is true to say that in general cathedrals have tended to stick to what they find easiest in offering the traditional diet of sermons, lectures and guided tours. The last two have much to commend them but, as they are generally offered, they suffer from too much concentration upon facts, many of which have little or no significance to life and faith. Generations of the imparting of facts in sermons, lectures and Sunday schools have not produced a Church which is strong. I believe that this is because, in sermons and lectures, not enough is done to explain the relevance of what is being said to the lives of those listening. Would that those responsible for preaching and teaching would have constantly in mind E. M. Forster's dictum, 'only connect'. The potential of guided tours for Christian education also remains largely unrealized: crucial links between the building, the Christian faith and people's experience are rarely made. Guided tours tend to concentrate almost exclusively upon the history and architecture of the building because those who volunteer for the task are particularly interested in this area. Equally importantly, there is a perceived exclusivity pertaining to cathedrals which means that they do not engage with the majority of the population. An ordinand on placement at Ely Cathedral produced a challenging report which drew attention to what he described as a virtual sign at the entrance of the cathedral which read: '*Sun* readers not welcome.'

It is difficult to articulate what it is about the ethos of cathedrals that makes them so apparently unwelcoming to large sections of the population but it is surely something to do with their association with 'high culture'. As Timothy Gorringe points out in his excellent *Furthering Humanity: A Theology of Culture*, when Paul Tillich came to elaborate a 'theology of culture' what he meant was 'the great works of the visual arts, of music, of poetry, of literature, of dance, of philosophy'.[6] Gorringe goes on to observe that:

> this list at once calls to mind the myriad works of 'high culture' spawned by the Christian faith and theology, the great cathedrals, mass settings and chorales, the canon of Western art from the eleventh to the twentieth centuries, the poetry of Donne, Herbert and Milton, of Edwin Muir and R. S. Thomas.

Worryingly for cathedrals and other purveyors of such 'high culture', Gorringe suggests that there has been a huge shift in what he refers to as the 'cultural dominant':

> The culture which was led by the market, 'the charts' and 'the top ten', only possible in the wake of the affluent society, came to define popular culture. What now became hegemonic was not 'high culture' symbolised by Reith's BBC, with its public service ethos, and its assumed role as guardian of public morals and as educator, but 'cultural populism'. This valorizes plebeian culture at the expense of high culture. High culture is elitist, conservative, snobbish, moralizing, paternalist. Popular culture is rooted in the ethos of the working or lower middle class, progressive, indifferent to status, non-judgemental in morals, tolerant of difference. The Church has suffered directly as a result of this cultural shift, being perceived as moralizing, judgemental, middle or upper class and out of touch. Attempts to create 'alternative worship' suffer both from a perception that they are cult-like, but also from the fact that they are not alternative at all, but an attempt to accommodate the cultural dominant.[7]

Ironically, it might be that cathedrals have thrived during the emergence of this new dominant culture precisely because they are seen as a bastion against it by the minority who patronize them. Certainly, some of those who come to worship in cathedrals do so because of what they perceive as the conservatism of cathedral worship. Many who visit do so for 'cultural' reasons similar to those who, for example, visit National Trust properties. There is a big question here about what cathedrals can do in order to engage with a greater proportion of the population. They are in a double bind not that dissimilar to that of the BBC. If they change what they offer in seeking to broaden their appeal, they will be accused of 'dumbing down'. If they remain as they are they will be berated for catering only for a small elite. It was awareness of this problem that led to the establishment of a project 'Cathedrals as Partners in Adult Learning'. It was the conviction of those who set up the project that cathedrals can and should work in partnership with other adult education providers in order to reach more people. The co-sponsor of the project was the National Institute of Continuing Adult Education and the Steering Group included people with considerable experience in adult education in the secular world. This group undertook surveys of adult education provision at cathedrals, and members of the Group visited every cathedral and organized conferences to agitate for better and more strategic adult education provision.

Some imaginative and constructive engagement with the problem has recently emerged. Estimates of the very high proportion of the population which had not darkened the doors of Norwich Cathedral, for example, led to the establishment of an initiative entitled 'Challenging Perceptions'. The overall aim of the project is to attempt to engage with a wider section of the community and to encourage greater accessibility through developing lifelong learning opportunities. The collaborative manner in which this project was developed in partnership with others attracted Lottery funding and enabled the appointment of a full-time outreach officer. This example shows that there can be a financial incentive for working with other agencies: grant-making bodies are more likely to look favourably upon applications which are made in partnership. In its first six months extensive networks with community workers and advisors across the city were created and a survey undertaken, with results collated by volunteers from the University of East Anglia. The latter showed an interest in the cathedral and in more public initiatives and these resulted in a 'Find Out Fair' which attracted 2,000 people and led on to other events. Work experience for long-term unemployed and marginalized people is being arranged both in Norwich and Ely, at the time of writing. Manchester Cathedral has played a leading role in urban and community regeneration in the city.

Such good practice will, I hope, be duplicated and improvised upon elsewhere, for there is a gospel imperative here. The mission of the Church of England in general and cathedrals in particular is to the whole of this land and it is essential that all opportunities be sought by cathedrals to reach out to every section of the communities in which they stand. Cathedrals, in general, have considerable contacts and they need to make use of them to entice people in – to visit and, if possible, to worship. Sometimes working with secular bodies to invite particular groups of people not just to visit but to worship can result in large numbers responding. One of the most moving types of service I have attended has been 'transplant' services for those who have in any way been involved with organ transplants – recipients, donors, relatives and medical staff. These are educational in the broadest sense in that they enable people to reflect upon their experience in a godly setting, which is what I have argued the education offered by cathedrals should be about. Similar services, including the traditional 'justice services', 'road peace' (organized for those who have been associated in any way with road traffic accidents) and volunteer services are organized in some cathedrals. All these enable similar reflection and assist human flourishing, the core aim of education. Many people make their way to cathedrals to light candles when tragedy strikes. Cathedrals are sometimes put in the same 'heritage' bracket as National Trust properties but this and much else make it clear that cathedrals have much more to offer. It is a moving experience to read the prayers left by those who have lit candles in cathedrals: it makes clear that they can enable deep feelings to surface and be articulated.

In the above and in much else there is, as I have indicated, a great deal of good practice to be found among the cathedrals in the field of adult education. The task ahead is not a sacrifice of all the things that cathedrals do well, in the name of 'popular culture', but a willingness to think and act imaginatively, creatively and prayerfully in order to produce a strategy to increase the cross-section of the population engaging with cathedrals. Cathedrals manage to attract huge numbers of young people without compromising their essential Christian witness. Using the experience gained there would do much to hone a strategy for work with adults. Cathedrals have the potential to act as cultural, educational and spiritual power houses for the dioceses and communities in which they are set. Much of that potential is being realized and there is a great deal for which to give thanks. My hope and prayer is that the ministry of cathedrals will blossom yet more as the twenty-first century progresses.

As they respond to the challenges of witnessing to an increasingly secular society with new and imaginative initiatives, one thing needs at all times to be borne in mind: cathedrals exist, first and foremost, to offer worship. In so far as they offer that worship, those who minister in them will, pray God, be inspired by the Holy Spirit to know what they should be doing. At the heart of this worship is the reading of the Scriptures encountered, daily and systematically, through the recitation of morning and evening prayer and the celebration of the Eucharist. If the Word of God is inscribed on the hearts and minds of those charged with ministering in the cathedral, it will confront and inspire, challenge and comfort them so that they can be enabled to do God's will. Further, if a cathedral is to reach its full educational potential, it must not just be a place where the few hear God's Word in the above services, it must be the home of a vibrant Christian community. A cathedral which is not will be a hollow edifice.

It is sometimes suggested that cathedrals should be 'centres of excellence'. I am uncomfortable with this notion since it can too easily be associated with the exclusive 'high culture' to which I have made reference above. However, cathedrals, and the communities of faith which are at their heart, should certainly be exemplary: they should be exemplary in worship, exemplary in welcome and exemplary in care. In so doing they should proclaim the love of God. At the beginning of this chapter I questioned the value of an exclusive concentration on the learning of facts in education. This fact, the supreme fact of God's love in Christ, cathedrals must do everything they can to proclaim for it is the only one, ultimately, that matters.

Notes

1 C. Dickens, *Hard Times*.

2 A. M. Allchin, *The World Is a Wedding* (London, Darton, Longman and Todd, 1978), p. 5.

3 A. Einstein, *Ideas and Opinions, based on Mein Weltbild,* ed. Carl Seelig (New York, Bonanza Books, 1954), p. 10.

4 A. McFadyen, *Bound to Sin* (Cambridge, Cambridge University Press, 2000), p. 6.

5 M. Booker and M. Ireland, *Evangelism – Which Way Now?* (London, Church House Publishing, 2003), p. 5.

6 T. Gorringe, *Furthering Humanity: A Theology of Culture* (Aldershot, Ashgate, 2004), p. 48.

7 Gorringe, *Furthering Humanity*, p. 56.

4

Liturgy on the frontiers: Laboratories for the soul

JEREMY FLETCHER

———◆◦◆———

> It is a Friday in January. Choral evensong, attended by around a hundred people, is coming to an end. The procession of choir and clergy emerges through the choir screen to face a huge stage, impressive PA system, video screens and a lighting rig. The band which will play at the Diocesan Youth Event in an hour's time is waiting to soundcheck. Tallis and Ebdon give way to rock, trance and house; the Book of Common Prayer to digital imagery. The dean and canons play a part in both, and each event is open to all.

The worship of the Church stands at the point of interplay between tradition and innovation. Every church which uses liturgical texts and structures brings the words of generations to the realities of the present and every church that reads the Bible brings words from three or more millennia to the beginning of a new millennium. In cathedrals this interplay is obvious because cathedrals act for the whole of the diocese; because they provide acts of worship on a daily basis; and because they are seen as places which function for the whole community. Those who plan and enact worship in such a setting cannot avoid the tension between the demands of inherited tradition and the varied requests of the day.

This chapter explores the ways in which today's cathedrals inhabit the frontiers of liturgy, worship and spirituality. For many years my view was that cathedrals were as far from the frontier as it was possible to be. Instead of being laboratories for the soul, they were shelters for the nostalgic: the liturgy was traditionally founded; the music was composed by the long dead; liturgical change hit cathedrals last, not first. The modern world might just be encountered – in a diocesan service by the inclusion of a 'modern' song or hymn, but still to the obvious distaste of the musicians and clergy. There are elements of truth here: that a cathedral exists on the frontier can be disturbing even for those who are travelling in the wagons. But the frontier is where we are, and there is more innovation than I would formerly have admitted.

Cathedral worship today

Certain styles of worship and liturgy have their natural home in a cathedral setting, but these are replicated in greater churches or collegiate communities (in the case of choral evensong), or in any church where the bishop is present (for example in the case of a 'parochial' ordination, or the blessing of oils). No act of worship is unique to a cathedral, and far from there being an obvious 'cathedral' style, today's institutions are characterized by a huge variety, which makes many parish churches seem narrow by comparison. My view of such worship was challenged first by my son's involvement as a chorister, and then by my work in a bishop's office. These last three years as Precentor have placed me squarely in the firing line since, on a daily basis, innovation and tradition collide on my desk. The worshipping frontier with which we engage is both broad and deep; the frontier is part of the trust deeds which give cathedrals their role and purpose. For this reason, it is worth reflecting in a little more detail on those things which are 'given' in a cathedral.

The shape of the frontier

Cathedrals put *daily worship* at the centre of their own work and witness. Every parish church is required to offer public daily prayer, and morning and evening prayer and the Eucharist on Sundays. Cathedrals do this proudly and publicly in a way that few churches can. In one sense this is done on behalf of those parishes and clergy who are unable to do so themselves. Typically most cathedrals spend well over 10 per cent of their budgets on worship, and the requirement of canons to be 'in residence' is one which normally demands their presence at daily acts of worship.

This daily round of worship is not simply an internal affair; a cathedral expresses both the *life of the diocese* and that of the *wider community*. It would be a strange cathedral which did not find itself being expected to host an ordination, the licensing of Readers and launches of various diocesan initiatives. During one month in York the same bishop found himself at a service with the laying on of hands for healing, a service for racial justice with steel bands and Asian dance, and at the Mothers' Union all-age celebration with action songs. Responding to the needs of the wider community can mean providing services which reflect community concerns, celebra tions of anniversaries and the annual offering of worship for long-standing groups. Every event is unique, and clergy and musicians can find themselves making some large cultural and liturgical leaps, often from one hour to the next.

A further complicating factor is the nature of the worshippers. For a variety of reasons people often find that cathedrals are *places of welcome* – strangers feel at home in a way that they might not in a smaller church. Our more culturally defined services (such as choral evensong) attract people who do not have the church experience or aesthetic equipment to inhabit them intelligently, yet who respond to them instinctively. Features of the frontier include both the *(in)experience of the worshippers* in core services and the interaction of the high points of the Christian worshipping life with people on the outer fringes of the life of faith. Most churches discover visitors at their services, but cathedrals know that on occasions the majority of worshippers will be 'outsiders'.

It is not the *type* of worship in a cathedral that defines the frontier. Many churches will, in their own context and in their own way, perform acts of worship that are at least similar, and in many ways are more radical. The defining characteristic of cathedral worship is the requirement for variety, the constant use by others, and the interaction of tradition and innovation. The cathedral's liturgical frontier is described therefore by the nature of the demand rather than by content.

Cathedrals in the lead

There is, of course, unimaginative and sloppy cathedral worship. One reaction to the perception of accelerating change is to retreat into the safety of the 'cathedral' style, as if it truly represents what has always been done everywhere and by everybody. In fact it is often the case that this style is unique to that particular institution, and probably dates only from the 1930s. So, York Minster currently sets its face against any kind of announcement at evensong, whereas it might be both courteous and helpful to offer some kind of welcome to a congregation which will never meet in that same way again. Style is a notoriously difficult thing to change.

Where opportunities have been embraced, cathedrals have been able to take a liturgical lead. A key area has been in the public use of the *Daily Office*. The daily pattern of prayer which is particularly evident in cathedral life has played its part in the creation of the Church of England's new office book. That regular daily pattern has ensured that there is both continuity and variety in what is now provided. Cathedrals have fluid communities, where a new congregation gathers to pray at the beginning and at the end of the day. Daily prayer requires a robust structure and a depth and quality of resource material, and the cathedral as an open and committed praying community is an excellent test bed for different patterns of prayer.

Daily prayer also brings with it the requirement to engage with the *psalms*. Reciting the psalms according to a fixed pattern derives from the early Church. It reached its classical Anglican form in Cranmer's table of psalms which uses all 150 in a month. Cathedrals embraced this with great devotion, but following the demise of sung daily matins can now find themselves struggling to use the morning psalms. Other patterns use the seasons of the year or the days of the week as a way of choosing psalms which are appropriate. We are not alone in looking for the best way to shape the use of the psalms, but finding new patterns while valuing the old has been a particular feature of recent cathedral life.

The same is true of the ordered daily use of the Bible. Recent *lectionaries* in the Church of England have used four continuous tracks of Bible reading during morning and evening prayer. Though this has the merit of covering much of the Bible in a year, it does not take into account the needs of the occasional attender at weekday evensong. A continuous pattern of Bible reading can be disconcerting to a large 'one-off' congregation, as those who have found themselves immersed in the depths of the book of Job while in the presence of 56 visiting Japanese know only too well. Out of this experience has come an attempt to provide readings which can 'stand alone' while relating to the Church's calendar. There is much to be said for a use of scripture which recognizes its role in public proclamation as well as being a pattern for regularly ordered study.

The Christian *calendar* is itself an act of mission. The Church gives a biblical shape to days and weeks in order to tell the world the Christian story. The Church's year provides the rhythm of daily and weekly worship in cathedrals. Since there is a daily worshipping community, however fluid, major feasts like Epiphany and All Saints can be celebrated on the day of the feast itself. Parishes which can only gather on a weekly basis will transfer the feast to the nearest Sunday. A community which has the capacity to use the calendar to its fullest extent is able to make the maximum use of all of its possibilities; bells ring and choirs sing for saints and anniversaries, for angels and apostles, for the Incarnation and the Resurrection. Expressing the full richness of the Easter and Christmas cycles, the saints and the founding events of our faith enables us to unfold the Christian story of faith to those who come through the doors.

The celebration of the *feasts* and *festivals* of the Church's year is where cathedrals feel most at home, and where experimentation and development take place most easily. This is especially true at Easter, where Palm Sunday processions, the washing of the feet and stripping of the altars on Maundy Thursday, elaborate liturgies for Good Friday, the Easter Vigil (either in the dark of Easter Eve or the dawn of Easter morning) and the great celebration of the Resurrection have spawned acts of worship offered to the whole church. *Lent, Holy Week, Easter* (1984) and *Common Worship: Times and Seasons* (to be published in 2006) were not exclusively written by precentors and deans. It is, however, from their use of such large spaces, with the accompanying expectation of spectacle and movement, that experimentation has produced liturgies which are transportable into the smallest and most parochial of contexts.

The *Easter Vigil* is perhaps the classic example of creative liturgy in a cathedral setting; indeed Portsmouth Cathedral was completed and reordered in the 1990s, partially with the Easter Vigil in mind. The

Easter fire is lit outside the building, with the congregation gathered in darkness. The new fire is carried in, the congregation gathers around the reading of the history of the people of God, and the Easter Candle is lit to loud proclamation. Ideally there is a baptism, and because of this many cathedrals are reassessing both the size of and the setting for their font. A procession of the whole congregation to the place of baptism is hugely effective: in York it is possible to descend into the crypt and then to ascend after the baptism and confirmation; this is a powerful expression of the baptismal movement of dying and rising in Christ. The congregation then gathers for Communion, before being sent away in peace, carrying the light of Christ. Those places which have a large Easter Garden often use this as a focus for the service. Some use different gardens to recall the gardens of Gethsemane, Calvary and the tomb. This should not be a 'lead case' enacted simply because of the available space: some kind of pilgrimage is possible in the smallest of places of worship, even if only for the candidates rather than the whole congregation.

The use of the Easter Vigil as the occasion of baptism and confirmation leads to a reflection on the role of the cathedral more widely in *initiation* in the diocese. The presence of a bishop for baptism and confirmation enables the pattern of initiation and Christian learning to be given a focus at the heart of the life of the diocese. It would be unfortunate if the bishop felt least at home in the church where his *cathedra* is placed. All should ensure that the means of enacting baptism and confirmation express the life of the diocese as focused in the mother church. A diocesan bishop who wishes to set the tone for baptism and confirmation throughout the diocese might well start with a decision about how to confirm 'centrally'. He can then decide how this form might be expressed appropriately in churches, communities and chaplaincies. An annual diocesan celebration where those recently baptized and confirmed could come to the cathedral would enhance the universal nature of initiation rather than making it a purely local event, and a connection between the two would strengthen both.

The life of the diocese is made manifest in many other ways. There are gatherings for diocesan services. As a precentor the first question I ask is 'who is in charge?' There is often a delicate balance to be struck between diocese, bishop and cathedral. Carefully managed, the tension can be intensively creative, symbolizing an understanding of the Church which both honours the bishop and expresses his relationship to his people. This is made possible by requiring him to be invited into the church where he is the principal minister, and valuing the place of clergy and laity in the decision-making of his diocese. Any diocesan service which takes place in the mother church is more than a one-off event: it speaks of the life of the diocese, its self-understanding and its mission. Some mutual 'giving way' is necessary: so, for example, an insistence on using the cathedral's musical resources alone might not be the most helpful for creating the right atmosphere in a healing service or racial justice event. Equally, badly amplified music groups do not always provide the best lead to a large congregation.

A similar process obtains when the service is being planned for another organization, such as a charity or interest group, a military or a civic organization. Such *'community' services* are the stock-in-trade of cathedrals. In this case, the first decision to be taken is whether the service and its contents are appropriate to the occasion and to the building. The hosting of an event by a cathedral invests it with a legitimacy it might not otherwise have had. The connection between the Church and the military life of the nation means that services for serving and former members of the armed forces are a matter of course, but occasionally it may be necessary to challenge a particular interpretation of events. The service in St Paul's Cathedral at the end of the Falklands War, where both Argentine and British service personnel were remembered, is a good precedent. The Church must always ensure that prayers and commemorations are appropriate to a Christian setting and Christian theology. This means valuing both justice and mercy; it also requires the Church to uphold the truth and point to the necessity of reconciliation and forgiveness. The flashpoint here can often be music. It will be up to individual institutions to decide whether 'Jerusalem', 'I vow to thee my country', 'O valiant hearts', or indeed something more avant garde, are appropriate or not.

The key theological principle is partnership. This is focused superbly well in the question which was asked by a precentor at Coventry Cathedral some years ago, when talking to any outside organization about a proposed act of worship. The precentor asked: 'What do you want to say to God?' This might well be followed up by its corollary: 'And what might God want to say to you?' It is easy for such an event to become a predictable collection of accessible hymns interspersed with readings chosen thematically, a non-biblical reading and an address or two. Beginning with the principle that such special services are means of theological communication, and that in the Incarnation God is to be found in the stranger, we should be prompted to bring significant imaginative resources to bear. How does this organization want to address God? What does it want to say to others about itself, given the Christian context of the service and setting? What does the Church wish to say here in the name of God?

Two examples will clarify the possibilities and dangers. An annual service for the Foundation for the Study of Infant Deaths in York has developed a form which expresses the mixture of mourning and thanksgiving felt by those who have lost children. Staff from the Foundation work with the recently and long-term bereaved, and encourage them to provide poems or readings which have been helpful in their despair. They are offered to be included in the service, and a rigorous editorial process means that the experience is not too traumatic, while being intensely personal for the reader. One such item started its life as a five-page essay. The end result was three paragraphs long, and very effective. The cathedral's contribution was to suggest the simplest of candle-lighting ceremonies, as a physical means of remembering. Because it is an annual service, we can regularly review the shape and the content. Because the organization works closely with its clients, it is possible to receive good feedback which contributes to the next year's service.

In contrast, a one-off service celebrating an anniversary for a Yorkshire women's association relied too much on the precentor's assumptions about what would take place. There were the usual hymns and prayers, but the address ended up as a fully-fledged attack on the Local Government Act 1974 and a strident call for the restoration of the Ridings of Yorkshire. Those who occupy the pulpit need to be aware of the responsibilities they bear, but the real lesson here was that the planning for this service was not rigorous enough, even if an altar call to join the fight would have received a one-hundred-per-cent response.

In the best places the worship which is developed for such special services can become a model which can be used by others. For example, the services planned for the fiftieth anniversary of the end of the Second World War, by St Paul's Cathedral, were offered to the wider Church and used enthusiastically. Since cathedrals are required to take the lead in these services it would be good if this model were used more frequently; there is too much local reinventing of the wheel.

In an ideal world this interaction changes the cathedral too. Depending on how defensive the dean and chapter may be, they can find themselves on the frontiers of liturgy which are already inhabited by others around them in the diocese and the Church nationally. At York, as in other places, the nave is emptied of chairs and furniture in January. The range of events which now make use of this flexible space illustrates the point very clearly: two diocesan youth events, an evangelistic ball and a Taizé service have broadened our normal programme. Hosting these events has changed the nature of our thinking about the celebration of Candlemas, such that elements from the Taizé celebration have contributed to a new style of service, using the empty nave as the launch pad for a different style of procession. To live on the frontier is to be changed by the experience as well as to bring one's own values into the encounter.

It should be impossible to imagine cathedrals without *movement*, *visual art* and *music*. Cathedrals might well be described as places of *procession*. Services such as the Stations of the Cross and Stations of the Resurrection have a natural home in such large spaces, and visitors to the building find themselves swept up into the movement. Processions within other services are also natural events: to the Lady Chapel on feastdays of the Blessed Virgin Mary, to altars dedicated to particular saints, and to tombs of important characters from the past history of the building or the region. But movement can also happen informally. At Ely different groups are encouraged to experience the building in the evening, with a musical accompaniment. Similar patterns have been used at Canterbury. At York, parish and deanery pilgrimage groups are conducted to different chapels and windows where appropriate hymns and prayers are used. In Norwich, children's groups are offered a pilgrimage liturgy, encountering different parts of the building and learning something of the Christian story. In Southwell the whole cathedral becomes a pilgrimage site for 5,000 children over a two-week period, and the event starts with a huge procession in through the west doors.

Though the buildings themselves are often referred to as testaments in stone, they are also places in which the best *art* can be utilized liturgically: in embroidery and banners, in altar frontals and furniture, in chalices and crosses. By this means art can be displayed for its own sake, for contemplation, reflection and appreciation. Some cathedrals have officers to promote the arts, and others seem to muddle through. But a thought-through commissioning policy with a desire only to use the best materials and design can leave a wonderful legacy for the next generation. The same is true of *music*, where a commitment to excellence means the commissioning of new work, and the training of musicians from the earliest age means a healthy flow of young people soaked in the music of Christian worship. In different settings in the British Isles some two thousand children lead the sung worship of the Church each week, and there is a valuing of children's gifts in cathedrals which can be mirrored in the wider Church to the benefit of all.

Running to catch up

On my noticeboard is an extract from an address to the Precentors' Conference some decades ago. It says that the only problem with the worship of cathedrals is the people. 'They will insist on turning up.' Tongue in cheek as it was, the underlying culture is not one which actually requires a regular *congregation*. A cathedral community is made up of employees, volunteers, regular attenders, occasional attenders, members of Friends organizations and the like. The community also includes those who give regularly but come hardly ever. There are so many 'stakeholders' that defining the 'members of the congregation' is a complex task. That makes things difficult for the people who have made the cathedral 'their church'. Both clergy and laity bring certain expectations to this encounter which the constitution, statutes and history don't always assist.

The great strength is that it is easy to attend a service in such a setting. Somehow the doors seem wide open, and the fact that many people come as tourists and have a warm view of the building seems to enable them and others to sit down in a service which they would not countenance attending elsewhere. The weakness is that this militates against the development of a congregational life which would be the norm in a parish setting. Regular worshippers in cathedrals have little history and experience of being part of a congregation; indeed they are often there because they have disliked congregational life in another place. Further irritations occur when the normal service is replaced by an ordination or 'county service', and when the regular congregation is thus displaced by the presence of invited guests. Just as the 9.30 a.m. congregation is beginning the process of gaining an identity, along comes the Legal Service or Battle of Britain Sunday and they have to disband for a week. But where the regulars embrace the vision, and welcome those who come once a year, there is great strength and a wealth of possibilities.

An additional difference between parishes and their mother church is the underlying culture of cathedral worship which requires congregations to *participate silently* and spiritually rather than actively. The prime example of this is choral evensong, where, in many places, the only words said by the congregation are those of the Creed. The commitment to excellent music performed by professionals means that in many places music is sung *for* rather than *by* the worshippers. Again, there are strengths and weaknesses here. It is easy to attend a service where all is done for you. But it requires a sophisticated spirituality to 'participate' in a service in which you 'do' very little, and the passive presence of the majority of worshippers does not say much for the interdependency of the Body of Christ. The question to ask is how a cathedral can make manifest the ministry of all the baptized while keeping most of its worshippers quiet.

New frontiers?

There is inertia and momentum, creativity and suspicion in the worshipping life of cathedrals. Occasionally these are very close together. For example, there are few examples of obvious *technological change* in most cathedrals. You will find few plasma screens or regular video projection in worship, but these do appear for special events. Many cathedrals, of course, have excellent public address systems and state-of-the-art lighting which offer imaginative possibilities. Durham's hugely popular Advent service makes use of a very sophisticated lighting system. Similarly, cathedrals produce their own individual orders of service in a way that acts as a model for parishes which now find that technology affordable and available. To take another example, traditionally cathedrals look on new musical expressions with a degree of suspicion. Nevertheless, they are also in the forefront of commissioning new pieces and can work at the edge of choral musical development, even where the guitar is seen as an instrument too far.

Exploration of new liturgical frontiers builds on existing strengths and creative thinking in cathedral life. New thinking about church growth has raised the possibility of churches *planting new congregations* within their existing building, defining those congregations by their style of prayer, music and participation. Cathedrals are ideally placed for this: easy to enter, they are used to providing services for distinct groups, and are well able to decide which resources are most appropriate for that particular service. Peterborough Cathedral began a service on a Sunday evening designed for 'returners' to church which used a journey through the building as a framework, and engaged with a group of people hitherto not represented in the cathedrals' regular clientele. The weekly life of a cathedral expresses the life of the Church in a multitude of forms, and this resonates with the Church's engagement with a world which is increasingly multicultural.

Stand in Salisbury, St Alban's, Truro, or any other cathedral, and you will see people not just visiting the building but also engaging with it as a place of prayer and worship. Many people symbolize their prayer by lighting a candle, and most also write their prayer down. Though the vast majority of people in the nation do not worship in a formal way on a regular basis, many are still able to express themselves spiritually. What is interesting is that the forms of worship generally provided in the same setting require liturgical and theological expertise at a level which would challenge most regular worshippers. This dislocation between hesitant visitors and liturgically accomplished 'insiders' is one with which cathedrals will need to engage. How can we work with those whose Christian knowledge is basic, whose worshipping experience is minimal, and yet who instinctively want to pray, to symbolize that prayer, and to encounter God in some way in such a building? It would be foolish simply to say that our regular worship should be simplified, as if 'dumbing down' was the answer; it is the very heightened and mysterious atmosphere of cathedral worship to which people find themselves responding. But this does not mean that all our language should be from the Authorized Version, and every prayer written in mock Tudor. Mystery is good; baffling people is not.

Another interesting question is whether people need to be present to participate. The fact that it is impossible to define exactly who belongs to a particular cathedral could offer exciting opportunities. The internet provides a way of circulating prayer material to the *dispersed community* of a cathedral, and some websites offer the opportunity for prayers from individuals to be posted. Making the monthly prayer list available, together with a form of prayer which mirrors that which is being used at morning or evening prayer each day, is a simple way of making a virtue of the fact that few people come every day, yet many people feel they belong. Sermons and parts of services can be posted in written form on a website, but MP3 files are available too. Cathedrals above all need to find ways of drawing their dispersed community together, even where this can lead to further dispersal: they are places of transit as well as stability.

Cathedrals are of course communities in their own right, yet they should also express something of *the life of the diocese*. Dioceses are inclusive and dispersed in their ministry and mission and so should their cathedrals be. Because they can attract people and events that would not be found in other churches, cathedrals can be used for expressions of worship and evangelism on behalf of the diocese. The cathedral which can host an Alpha supper, arrange an Emmaus teaching course, be a venue for Café Church and host an alternative worship event will be enabling the diocese to be a unit of mission. The historic connection between cathedral ministry and education means that the role of adult learning, evangelism and the catechumenate is another golden opportunity. A diocese might well consider how to make the cathedral a centre for Christian initiation and discipleship. The connection between the cathedral, the role of the bishop and the inclusion of new disciples is one which will generate new patterns of worship and instruction which can be a model for churches across the diocese.

The frontier which cathedrals currently inhabit is that between the Church and organizations and causes working across the wider community. The challenge here is to welcome groupings which are representative of an increasingly non-Christian society in a manner which is both inclusive yet is also clear about the claims of the Christian faith. This works in a number of ways. As the largest meeting place in York, the Minster is asked whether events can take place which have no overtly Christian content, and which occasionally contain elements which are neo-pagan or are from other faiths. Some Christian interest groups whose values are opposed by other Christians will wish to worship. Within the Chapter in York we have discussed the regular use of the building by a group which wrote up its activities in a journal, congratulating the cathedral on allowing 'pagan worship'. An art installation by an avowed pagan also attracted press comment. In many ways a cathedral is at its best when it is a market place for ideas and causes which can exist in a safe space and take their place in a multicultural setting. There are limits, however, and the Dean and Chapter will have to decide whether a stated desire to be inclusive allows an organization to pray overtly to another deity or to dance in a way which invokes the ancient fertility gods of the land. At what point does the gospel of love draw a line in the sand? The frontier can be an uncomfortable place on which to live.

The edge is the centre

Ultimately cathedrals are places of welcome and transformation. Nowhere is this more true than of their worship. Their very construction points to the existence of a God of mystery and awe, yet in their nooks and crannies are places of intimacy and comfort, where the hesitant can light a candle and say a prayer. Where it has been easy for individuals to make the 'vertical' connection between themselves and God, it has been more difficult for the 'horizontal' connection between people to be developed. Worship which makes much of mystery and reverence can find communion between people difficult to express. Perhaps the regular diet of worship will remain much the same in this regard, yet the fact that people feel welcomed, that they feel that the building is public as well as sacred space, will allow worship provided on those occasions to open up the possibilities of connection between people. Our worship will be at its most challenging when mystery and inclusion coincide. Nobody so welcomed should leave unchanged.

5

Glory and pride:
The Church and its cathedrals

CHRISTOPHER LEWIS

❦

Pride

That the Church is ambivalent about its cathedrals is not cause for surprise. Institutions, especially ones which are perceived as large, attractive and mysterious, evoke strong feelings. Cathedrals are symbols of divine inspiration and hope, yet also known for pride and intrigue. Although apparently eternal, they cost a fortune to keep in good repair. While welcoming visitors, they can behave as arcane societies bent on their own designs.

Novels are written about cathedrals because the tension between transcendent purpose and worldly endeavour provides a ready seam to mine: dark forces struggle with beautiful worship, the vagaries of a confined community are coupled with public exposure. And is there not (as a character in a Victorian novel remarks) quite apart from the gossip of a cathedral close also a great waste of energy?[1] What is the point of it all? Is the small addition to God's glory worth the effort? Anthony Trollope is often quoted, but that is much in the manner that people refer to Evelyn Waugh when wanting to summon up the worst (or nostalgic best) in an ancient university. Strange tribal antics, half lost in the mists of time, provide good ammunition for the critics and sometimes role models for those in search of something quaint. A more profound and pessimistic picture is painted by William Golding in his novel, *The Spire*, which tells of the passion of a medieval dean to build the 400ft crowning glory for his cathedral, come what may: 'Remember this is my house, under God.' The cathedral close is his kingdom, a theocracy, a religious fiefdom within which the dean's designs are bound to prosper for they are identical to those of God.

In *The Spire*, everything is made subservient to the overriding aim of the upward extension of the building: no letters are answered that are not connected with the spire, for the project is supreme. The wonderful building is seen as a Bible in stone, a diagram of prayer, a sermon, with the angels on its side and opponents dismissed as lacking faith. So the dean:

> The earth is a huddle of noseless men grinning upward, there are gallows everywhere, the blood of childbirth never ceases to flow, nor sweat in the furrow, the brothels are down there and drunk men lie in the gutter. There is no good thing in all this circle but the great house, the ark, the refuge, a ship to contain all these people and now fitted with a mast.

But then disaster approaches and the dean, a broken man, sees the error of his ways: 'I thought I was doing a great work; and all I was doing was bringing ruin and breeding hate.' The foundations, literal and spiritual, are not sufficient to the task. And was the task the right one anyway?[2]

'The great house, the ark, the refuge, a ship': what is the Church? There is debate, of course, as to whether Jesus (like many of his followers) thought the world would soon end and therefore that the work of founding an institutional Church was superfluous. In that case, to have a few followers was desirable, loosely arranged to spread the word, but with the Temple destroyed or about to be, the politics of continuity were not at the top of the apostles' list. When Jesus spoke of the Temple, it was not to wax lyrical about the abounding grace of sacred space but rather to forecast the Temple's demise. He himself left no monuments. And the Temple was indeed destroyed, never to be rebuilt. Perhaps the model for the Church was more that of the guerrilla group, flexible and responsive, than that of the hierarchy which came into being after the conversion of the emperor Constantine, with its local expressions throughout the known world.

The world, however, did not end and, as Max Weber and other sociologists have pointed out, charisma is hard to perpetuate. Eventually the pure, small group either disintegrates or, alternatively, has to give itself shape in terms of both people and places. What had been peripatetic settles and puts down roots; the inspired group gathered around the wandering preacher discovers that it needs buildings to live in and rules by which it can govern itself. As the years pass, it may develop a longing for Gothic architecture and the associated financial paraphernalia. Charisma is gradually transmuted into routine, although the traffic is not all one way, for new and reforming movements may seek to rediscover the original purity. The Benedictines were the revolutionaries in their day. Then they settled down with the rule and their farms and, in the view of some, became effete; the Cistercians followed and reformed what had gone before.

Throughout the history of the Church, its theology of itself has interacted with actual arrangements on the ground; there is no special priority of theological thought over practical action, since the guidance given in the biblical and other sources for theologies of the Church (ecclesiology) is not exactly a blueprint. The Church has to 'work' and numerous models have been tried by Christians. The Bible contains many different images of the Church and, although some such as 'the body of Christ' are employed extensively in liturgy and theology, each model is only partial and will need to be supplemented and 'reformed' by others. What is learned from biblical images is that there should be 'no obsession with one image, but a new freedom in the use of many'.[3] A model which implies the settled and corporate may need the insights of more dynamic models (such as 'the people of God') or more mysterious ones ('the bride of Christ').

Glory

'The ark, the refuge, a ship': there is no doubt that cathedrals have their origin in a particular period, one where these great ships declared the power of God and of the Church, speaking of stability and religious certainty in an age of political flux. Great things went on around them in medieval times and their economic and political role was intertwined with the religious. Their origins are often monastic: as centres of power, good works, worship and land management. Then, after the Dissolution of the Monasteries in England, cathedral constitutions spelled out their independence, not least from the bishop who had his 'seat' there but otherwise had only limited rights; diocese and cathedral were and are economically and structurally largely distinct. That cathedrals survived the Reformation at all is remarkable, for what was to be their new function in a post-monastic age? Survival was due in part to the fact that the new religious order retained much of the pre-Reformation culture, but also because cathedrals were seen to have a continuing purpose in that their role as the seat of the bishop and as places of prayer and learning was complementary to the work of the parishes. Some, like Thomas Cranmer, had doubts, but the cathedrals continued and managed to adapt themselves, if slowly. 'The people of post-Reformation England found that they had got cathedrals: they didn't quite know why, but they made the best of them – they made them into vibrant, characterful contributors to Christian life and worship.'[4]

What then is their place in the Church today, in a Western world which has changed markedly from the time that gave birth to most cathedrals? There are a number of roles that they have, but the most distinctive and fruitful is exactly in the area discussed in this chapter, namely, in their model of what it is to be the Church. It is in being the Church in a creative way that their glory lies.

The central paradox is that the very buildings which look most static and traditional are in fact among the most flexible when it comes to being the Church in the contemporary Western world. The paradox depends on the cathedrals' capacity to be both sacred and public spaces. There are other associated paradoxes: the most ecclesiastical of buildings (being the seat of the bishop) has also the ability to be the most 'neutral' of religious spaces, with the capacity for creative use for ecumenical and indeed for interfaith purposes. The most apparently enclosed can be the most accessible. The most traditionally Christian can be attractive and religiously stimulating to those who live in a post-Christian (but not post-spiritual) culture. These paradoxes rest in part on size and accessibility, in part on dedication to a God who is not, as it were, a particularly partisan God.

Noah's ark contained every kind of creature, so perhaps that is a good image with which to start. That picture, however, needs to be complemented by others, for images focus our experience in a new way; in a cathedral, images are needed which help to express the firm

Christian centre yet also the accessible and open nature of the perimeter. So perhaps body, Temple and flock become less evocative, whereas field, new creation and vine (or indeed new and non-biblical images like café, beacon or oasis) become more so. What the Church is in essence is a mystery, so more than one image will be necessary in any exploration of its nature. What is more, each image has implications and there is no doubt that the idea of the Church exemplified in cathedrals is better expressed by open images than by more closed ones.

A difficulty with much contemporary discussion of the Church is that it only works with two models: either the community or the association. The more settled, traditional and, by implication, rural community is compared with new, flexible, 'postmodern' forms of religious arrangement which are seen as novel ways of being the Church. These latter associational gatherings relate less to place and more to specific kinds of interest and activity. It follows that evangelism moves from a model based on geographical roots to one which aims to attract new members to a network.[5]

What such analysis overlooks is the ability of institutions which appear to be naturally allied to community thinking to reinvent themselves so that they also provide floorspace and impetus to more associational ways of being the Church. In other words, different models can coexist and readily do so in a cathedral. Flexible networks do not necessarily have to be set up in free-floating contexts; indeed, as has already been pointed out, they may rapidly wither if they do not attend to continuity. Being part of a network can be combined with being a member of a communion. If much contemporary religious practice is characterized by religious belief without institutional belonging, then the most suitable religious expression on the ground may be the kind of cross between association and community found in cathedrals: a cellular model with a number of different ways of being the Church interacting in one place.

How does contemporary society in the West get in touch with the sacred? The answer is: in a wide range of ways. Outside Europe, the expressions of religion are in general more institutional, but in the West, with its inheritance of state-sponsored religion, the response in the new age is diffuse. It is the spirituality of Glastonbury Tor, a hill with a history and with mystical associations that make it a holy place in many people's view. Anyone has access; one has only to climb the hill, or, if feeling less energetic, to approach it and contemplate. In contrast to the Tor, the picture presented by much of the Church is that of closed circles of devotees with their backs to the world, busying themselves being 'the body of Christ'. The pattern may be eucharistic, a service packed with symbolism and profound meaning for the committed Christian, but often impenetrable to the uninitiated. Or it may be the charismatic gathering, the Bible study group or morning worship in a country church. These are all expressions of what it is to be Christian, but that is not the issue here. The question is to find ways in which people can be in touch with the sacred and then discover something of the Christian faith.

In Gregory Baum's book on twentieth-century theology, he comments on an essay by Harvey Cox. The essay

> suggests that the secularising trend of the twentieth century is being left behind by an extraordinary revival of religion: a living encounter with the sacred at the edge of the churches and the traditional religions. The religious feeling of contacting the divine is so powerful and spiritually liberating that it makes liberation in the material sense a secondary issue – desirable, yes, but on a lower level than the living contact with the sacred.[6]

Those comments may be influenced by their North American context, but the phrase 'encounter with the sacred at the edge of the churches' chimes in with other, more European, analyses of religious belief and activity.

Liminal space

The Church is often described by its beliefs, its organization, its purposes; but what of its edges? If there is to be 'encounter with the sacred at the edge of the churches' then the boundary merits close attention. To use the traditional theological categories: what is 'Church' and what is 'world'? It is the porch, the threshold or the margin which have a particular place in the Christian tradition for they are crucial for contact with the world around. Yet they are insecure areas, what the anthropologists call 'liminal', for they signify transition and uncertainty, openness to possibility.[7] Are you in or are you out?

Cathedrals are more loved by the world than by the Church. To the Church they often seem to be engaged in some ancillary business, more concerned with city, county and the wider world than with the affairs of the Church. Their worshippers may prefer anonymity and be hard to define in terms of their allegiance. Their visitors are even harder to place: the half tourist, half pilgrim who comes in the guise of a consumer, buys a postcard, lights a candle, gazes at an arch, pins up a prayer, even sits on the edge of worship and then goes home. Cathedrals run services for secular groups: a local factory, a bowls club, the local council, a regiment, those caught up in a train crash, to take examples from a particular cathedral.

What cathedrals provide is the opportunity for people to explore and perhaps to cross the awkward boundary between the secular and the sacred and to handle the insecurities of liminality. That is a function within (and outside) the Church. To put it another way, the cathedral provides common ground of a particular kind on which people can roam or pasture at will, much as sheep graze on a common. That may be why so many 'odd' people of one kind or another tend to gravitate towards cathedrals; they find a safe and welcoming place in which they are helped to grow in faith and confidence. It is a boundary experience and also may be a boundary-crossing one. The key point about a common is its accessibility (it follows that charging to enter cathedrals is likely to compromise their work) and important battles have been fought with landowners in order to stop them enclosing common land. There is a right to roam on a common. Common ground, which is kept common by its dedication to God, is of supreme importance in modern Europe, both because of general ignorance of the beliefs of the Church, but also because religion is perceived as being a private affair, impenetrable to those whose faith is in doubt. How can a visitor have free access to a Church which speaks a private language in a private place and demands particular and identifiable signs of commitment from its members? In an age which the churches label as 'secular', their reaction is often to assume that religious activity must be for the obviously converted and therefore intense, but the idea of 'the common' runs counter to that trend and signals a broader understanding of the Church.

That wider perception is why the cathedral is often the natural place for ecumenical worship: it is to some degree outside particular church allegiance and therefore a place where boundaries can be explored. An extension of the same point makes for interfaith opportunities, for faiths other than the Christian can often relate to the public and sacred space of a cathedral as neutral territory on which real contact can be made. A cathedral which had a serious fire received a deputation from the local mosque on the following day, which came to deliver a collection made towards the repairs. The cathedral was for them a sacred place in whose troubles they felt involved.

Cathedrals are (or should be) places for the best kind of Christian risk. The ecumenical experiment, the interfaith event, the exploration of the boundaries of religious art or music: all these have their place within its generous walls. No cathedral filing system is complete without a good collection of letters of comment, complaint and congratulation after events which test the religious or artistic perimeter which has been set by Church convention. A domesticated cathedral is a sorry thing.

The base camp

To describe the cathedral's role in this way is not to say that other aspects of the Church are of lesser significance, but merely that cathedrals complement (and overlap with) their work. Although boundary explorations are crucial to the cathedral, the continuity with the Church's work is considerable.

The prime, specifically ecclesiastical, purpose of a cathedral is to provide both a symbolic and a real home for the bishop of the diocese. Here is his or her seat and the cathedral would not be a cathedral without it. The bishop and the cathedral together are the main symbols of a diocese; whether they like it or not, they have a representative role. In the cathedral he or she should feel welcome, doubly so as the bishop can relax, knowing that responsibility for running it lies with the dean and canons. Here there is the opportunity for the bishop to preach, to teach, to hold conferences and special services. Here the comparatively small events which are often the experience of Christians can be complemented by large gatherings for particular purposes. No cathedral in England can match Cologne which has a capacity of nine or ten thousand, but most have the space for major services and the experience to organize them. To go to 'the cathedral' for an event means that it is special and memorable, which explains why there are heightened expectations of a visit there and heightened disappointment if they are not met.

The cathedral can also act as a suitable base camp for others who work primarily in the diocese or in the wider Church. It may be right that some officials emerge from a diocesan office block, but that means that they are associated with administration. Those who are engaged, for example, in clergy training, in mission or in Christian social responsibility have often found it creative to work from a cathedral. Here is a community with whom to worship and pray; here are facilities which can be used in their work; here is a particular kind of church with which it is helpful to be linked. There is a long tradition in cathedrals, not only of a community gathered around the building, but also of the cathedral as 'minster', the place from which people go out to do the work of the Church and to which they return.

The cathedral can thus be a resource for the Church. The clergy are often available to preach. Training courses may meet at the cathedral, and imaginative religious and other education may be arranged for children and for adults. Music of all kinds, secular and religious, has a special place in cathedrals, for singers and other musicians are usually a high priority in the life of the place and in the budget. To mention music raises the possibility that the cathedral not only asks people to come to it to use its resources, but also takes the resources out to churches and others. It may be expensive for professional musicians and educationalists to go on tour, but it is desirable that the cathedral's expectation is not solely that people will come to it. There can be a mobile cathedral, deploying its resources where they are needed.

Good practice is not always easy to communicate from a cathedral because standards and styles (for example, in music) vary so greatly, but there are many cases of imaginative work, where the cathedral interacts creatively with the rest of the Church.

For all the people

Cathedrals perch on the edge, between Church and world. Their roots go right back to that strange and ambiguous event, the conversion of the emperor Constantine. For then the Church became, in intention at least, one with the world and it constructed great buildings as a sign of its presence and its power. The sacred and the secular coexisted and indeed were intertwined; the Church did not have to define itself over against the world, for the boundaries were not of particular importance. Yet the world of religion is ever changing and now the tide of Church membership and attendance has receded in Europe, while the waters of the Spirit have flowed in unconventional directions.

The picture is complex and means that the model of the Church which Christians employ is of crucial importance: ecclesiology comes to the fore. If the world outside the Church is seen as pagan and sinful, then the tendency will be to draw the boundaries tight and to shelter Christians from the cold winds without. That picture is the one which many sociologists and theologians would have painted 30 years ago, at the time of writing, and it takes a long time for views to change. Now, however, the evidence does not seem to be pointing in the direction of that picture. Worldwide, religion is burgeoning to the extent that the sociologist Peter Berger has written of 'desecularization' and said that the world is 'as furiously religious as it ever was, and in some places more so than ever'.[8] In Europe the evidence is different, and seems to point to a more diffuse religious pattern, with much spirituality, little church attendance and yet an expectation that religious institutions carry on with a vicarious role and are there for emergencies.[9]

Changes in society might have left cathedrals like whales on a beach. The evidence points, however, to new life and new roles. The first role is to have a different, more inclusive, and indeed prophetic understanding of the Church when compared with much of Christianity today. To be a model of what the Church could be, is a crucial task: inclusive moderation in a time of religious extremism and comprehensiveness at a time of social fragmentation. Without possessiveness, cathedrals can be for all the people: places of ebb and flow, set apart in the name of God as common ground and therefore both sacred and public at the same time. They can be a great resource to the daily life of the Church, and yet they point outwards, for otherwise they would not be able to perform the function of being 'our cathedral' for quite so many people.

Notes

1 V. L. Whitechurch, *The Canon in Residence* (London, Fisher Unwin, 1904), p. 130.

2 William Golding, *The Spire* (London, Faber, 1965), pp. 40, 106, 209.

3 P. S. Minear, *Images of the Church in the New Testament* (London, Lutterworth, 1961), p. 251. He counts 96 images of the Church in the New Testament.

4 Christopher Haigh, *Why Do We Have Cathedrals? A Historian's View* (Perth, St George's Cathedral, 1999), p. 14.

5 An example is *Mission-shaped Church: Church Planting and Fresh Expressions of Church in a Changing Context* (London, Church House Publishing, 2004) (a Church of England report).

6 Gregory Baum, *The Twentieth Century: A Theological Overview* (New York, Orbis, 1999), p. 248. Harvey Cox's essay is called 'The Myth of the Twentieth Century: The Rise and Fall of Secularisation'.

7 For example, in Victor Turner, *The Ritual Process* (London, Routledge, 1969).

8 Peter Berger, *The Desecularization of the World* (Grand Rapids, William B. Eerdmans, 1999), p. 2.

9 See Grace Davie, *Europe – the Exceptional Case* (London, Darton, Longman and Todd, 2002).

6

Joining Athens with Jerusalem: Cathedrals and universities

STEPHEN PLATTEN

———◆•◆◆•◆———

'I fancy we have had enough of Jerusalem,' Sue said, 'considering we are not descended from the Jews. There was nothing first rate about the place, or people, after all – as there was about Athens, Rome, Alexandria and other old cities.'[1]

Typical dialogue from the tortured Sue Bridehead in Hardy's *Jude the Obscure*. *Jude* is a harrowing but fascinating book. It was Hardy's last novel. The outcry it provoked both from Emma, his wife, and from wider society helped decide him to shift to that very different and sometimes more opaque genre of poetry. Some see *Jude* as Hardy's best novel; others see it as overwritten. This ought not to be surprising, since, of all his novels, *Jude* has more of Hardy himself in it than any of the others. And this, remembering that every one of his novels is influenced significantly by his own experience and psychology. *Jude*, however, touches most deeply upon Hardy as a person. His hurt through the snobbery of Victorian society and notably through the Church; his further confusion in matters of faith; his earlier desire to be ordained himself.

In *Jude*, much of this is focused early on in attitudes to learning. Here, once again, Hardy's insecurities are exposed. He never forgot his comparatively short academic career and his brief apprenticeship as an architect. The chapters set in Christminster (Oxford) focus this particularly sharply. Its significance as a centre of learning is amply demonstrated in the text, but it is a place closed to him: 'When the gates were shut, and he could no longer get into the quadrangles, he rambled under the doorways, feeling with his fingers the contours of their mouldings and carvings.'[2] It was also the place where the perplexities of faith had been most rigorously exposed. He mentions Keble and quotes Newman's *Apologia*:

> My argument was . . . that absolute certitude as to the truths of natural theology was the result of an assemblage of concurring and converging probabilities . . . that probabilities which did not reach to logical certainty might create a mental attitude.[3]

Hardy also notes that Christminster is a cathedral city:

> From his window he could perceive the spire of the cathedral, and the ogee dome under which resounded the great bell of the city.[4]

Here then is Hardy's classical picture of learning, in the place where, uniquely, cathedral and university come together, even under one roof. It is in *Jude* too that Melchester (Salisbury) looms large and, once again, cathedral and learning stand side by side. Jude continues to explore his vocation to the priesthood in Melchester and Sue goes there to attend Melchester Normal School,[5] that is, the training college for teachers.

Hardy's literary pictures, then, of both Oxford and Salisbury bring together cathedrals and academies in the specific way in which they overlapped in Victorian England. It is a particular view, of course, but it identifies resonances which extend well back beyond the limits of the nineteenth century and, indeed, the coasts of the British Isles, although the English cathedral links are unique. Those links point back specifically to the vast growth in the Benedictine life during the medieval period. The impact of this expansion had marked consequences for the cathedrals in England.

The remarkable growth of the monasteries across the continent in the twelfth century would ultimately effect vast changes upon European culture. Not least, there was the Benedictine influence on learning.[6] Learning is integrally related to listening, and to the Benedictine keynote of obedience, which comes from a related Latin root meaning to 'listen intently'. The Prologue to Benedict's Rule begins: 'Listen my son to the instructions of your Master, turn the ear of your heart to the advice of a loving father.'[7] The Prologue continues: 'We propose, therefore, to establish a school of the Lord's service, and in setting it up we hope we shall lay down nothing that is harsh or hard to bear.'[8] Elsewhere in the Rule there are clear indicators that, at the very least, the monks will read and study the Scriptures. In a later chapter it is noted that: 'during these days of Lent everyone should receive a book from the library, which he should read from the "beginning".'[9] This focus upon learning spread broadly across the monasteries; in contemporary imaginative literature monks and their libraries have also left their marks.[10]

Even a superficial glance at the ancient universities of Europe identifies the marks of the monastic life. The quadrangles in the universities of Krakow in Poland, of Florence in Italy, and of Salamanca in Spain all recall the monastic origins of European universities. It was a migration of monks from the Sorbonne in Paris that led to the foundation of the University of Oxford; a further migration from Oxford was the seed for the growth of the University of Cambridge. Colonies of monks continued to have their own place in both these universities. The badges of Benedictine monasteries (including that of Norwich Cathedral) can still be seen at Worcester College, Oxford (an inheritance from its predecessor Gloucester Hall). Trinity College, Oxford, was formerly Durham College, founded by the Benedictine monks of that cathedral, and Magdalene College, Cambridge, too was rooted in colonies of Benedictine monks.

We can now see the emerging links between English cathedrals and the universities in the medieval period. We referred to the uniqueness of the English cathedral tradition. This relates to the monastic nature of a number of the ancient cathedrals. Canterbury, Durham, Ely, Norwich, Rochester, Winchester and Worcester were all founded jointly as monasteries and cathedrals. Gloucester and St Albans, which were made cathedrals respectively in the sixteenth and nineteenth centuries, also have Benedictine roots. Carlisle was an Augustinian priory. Also, in the sixteenth century, the new cathedral in Oxford was set in Christ Church; here was the shrine of St Frideswide, an eighth-century religious. In 1096, when Herbert de Losinga founded the cathedral in Norwich, he also founded a school. Other monastic cathedrals, notably Canterbury, similarly had parallel foundations set up for learning.

We need neither to labour this argument, nor to attempt to prove too much by means of it. The evidence makes it clear that the great flowering of the Benedictine way not only influenced the growth of learning within European culture, it also was a key element in the growth of the university tradition and the handing on of the seven liberal arts. Furthermore, we can see how, in England, the confluence of the monastic and cathedral traditions spilled over into the foundation of the ancient universities. Cathedrals had a stake in education, both through this and through the establishment of parallel educational foundations alongside them. Many of the medieval cathedrals developed substantial libraries which became a resource for the wider community of learning. Grace Jantzen, in her classic study of Mother Julian, mentions the excellence of the Norwich Cathedral priory library.[11] Adam Easton, a monk from that same priory, rose to become a great scholar and a curial cardinal in Rome.

The Reformation took its toll of cathedrals, as it did of other institutions, within the Church. Libraries were sometimes broken up and the contents lost; often the abbey or priory rolls were destroyed. In some places – Hereford is the prime example with its chained library – the marks of scholarship remained. It is, however, to the nineteenth century, and to the period of the foundation of new universities, that we should now leap. How did the Church of England and its cathedrals respond? The nineteenth century became increasingly a period of great educational reform within England. Unlike Scotland, with its four ancient university foundations at Aberdeen, Edinburgh, Glasgow and St Andrews, England still had just the two collegiate universities centred in Oxford and Cambridge. These two universities would themselves eventually be reformed, notably in the acts of 1854 and 1856, which opened them up, in terms of lower degrees, to people of any religion, or none. The broadening of fellowships, making them available to anyone and not just clergy, came later; the opening up of the ancient universities to women had to wait until the twentieth century.

In the late 1820s, largely owing to the energy of Jeremy Bentham and his Utilitarian enthusiasts, pressure emerged to establish more university places. The result of this was the establishment first of University College, London, in 1824, an entirely secular foundation, tagged immediately by its opponents 'the godless institute of Gower Street'; to this day the embalmed body of Bentham, its founding father, can be viewed on application. Bentham's gift of his own corpse was an intriguing symbol of his Utilitarian beliefs. Even his body, after his death, might be a useful and practical object for the study of science and the edification of humanity. It is said that the mummified look on his face reflects the seriousness of his character and the intensity of his personality. As a counter to the apparent advance of secularism, King's College, London, was established by forces within the Church of England in 1828.

It was in 1832, however, with the foundation of the University of Durham (on collegiate lines) that cathedrals and universities once again began to exercise a mutual influence upon each other. Durham, before the days of cathedral reforms, was a particularly eccentric foundation. It was infested with pluralisms. So, for example, the Bishop of St David's was the Dean, and he had, as some of his fellows on the chapter, the bishops of Bristol, Chester and Exeter. Alongside these, there were nine other canons, all of whose stipends were substantial. The Bishop of Durham was also in receipt of considerable income. Admittedly, at the time, the palatine powers of the see still survived to some extent, and so he had other officials to pay. Nevertheless, it was clear that the secular powers might, in due course, wish to divert these revenues to be used for other purposes. Utilitarianism was in the air!

It was this, among other things, that persuaded the chapter to use some of these revenues for 'higher education in the context of the Christian religion'. Ironically, the University of Durham was founded in 1832, the year of the Great Reform Bill, which was piloted by Lord Grey, who also had impeccable Northumbrian connections. Certainly it was not coincidental that the move came in the same year as the Reform Bill. It is unclear who first suggested the idea of a university. One of the prebendaries, a Dr Durell, wrote to Bishop van Mildert warning him of the advances of reform.[12] Van Mildert himself was clear that any move toward founding a university should not be simply on the grounds of expediency, but that it should also be for the greater good of education. In the event, the chapter made their decision on 28 September 1831 to institute Durham College. It cannot be said that they took the decision with enthusiasm. The proposal ran into further difficulties when it was discovered that the degrees of the university would be open – as with the ancient universities – only to members of the Church of England by law Established. If degrees were to be awarded to people other than members of the Church of England, then the scheme would not be laid before Parliament. In the event, those opposing the initiative fell back and the parliamentary process culminated in the royal assent on 4 July 1832, just one month after the passing of the Great Reform Bill.

The issue of the relationship of universities to both the Established Church and to the Christian religion became increasingly a key issue both in the development of the universities and in the implications that this would eventually have in the development of the cathedrals of England. The foundation of the University of Durham posed similar questions. Even so, out of this mixed economy of political expediency and educational high-mindedness was born only the second new university in England since the Reformation, indeed since medieval times. The links between the cathedral and the university survive. The dean remains the only non-university employee who is ex-officio on the university council. Interestingly enough, during the Commonwealth period, Oliver Cromwell had initiated plans which became fairly well advanced to inaugurate a new university. It was to have been in Durham, and it was intended to be an Oxbridge of the north, centred on the cathedral; Cromwell would, after all, have had no other use for the cathedral.

As we have already seen, religious tests became one of the key elements in the controversy over the broadening of educational provision in the latter part of the nineteenth century. Early in the century two rival organizations, aimed at increasing *school* provision, had been set up: Dissenters had founded the British and Foreign School Society in 1812, although the roots of that initiative with Joseph Lancaster went back as far as 1801; in parallel and, indeed, in competition with this, was established the National Society for Promoting the Education of the Poor in the Principles of the Established Church. This was formally set up in 1811, and, in a very different guise, still exists today. It was, however, in the wake of the 1870 Forster

Education Act that competition and controversy reached a peak in the final three decades of the nineteenth century.[13] This was also the period during which the so-called civic (later known as 'redbrick') universities were being set up, largely in the north of England. It coincided too with the birth of Fabian socialism, and with those energies which led to the foundation of the Workers' Education Association (WEA) in 1903. Many of these initiatives were, at the very least, suspicious of the Established Church, and the cathedrals were seen as symbolic of its dominant and privileged position. Ironically, this is not true of the WEA itself, whose founder, Albert Mansbridge, was a highly committed member of the Church of England. Mansbridge was caught up into both the University Extension Movement and the Church of England Tutorial Classes. The extension movement also had establishment backing.

Nonetheless, the real growth in the establishment of the precursors of the civic universities issued from three rather different, and sometimes opposing, sources. Those three sources were dissent, the Mechanics' Institutes (here the roots can even be traced back into the late eighteenth century, with Robert Owen's experiments at New Lanark in Scotland and New Harmony in the USA) and also industrial patronage. The universities of Huddersfield, Sheffield, Leeds and Birkbeck College, London, trace their origins to the Mechanics' Institutes. Manchester, Sheffield and Birmingham benefited from industrial philanthropy. Joseph Chamberlain, a Unitarian and an industrialist, gave money to the embryonic University of Birmingham, thus bringing together the twin influences of dissent and industry. At this point there was little conflict between the growth of university education and either the Church of England or the Christian faith more widely. Nonetheless, there was a shift in ethos. Each of these university colleges had strong schools of applied science, and there was a move away from the ideal of a classical education. This may well have contributed to a transformation in the relationship between the Christian religion and the universities later in the twentieth century.[14] Indeed, there was even a history of persecution of liberal churchmen going back to the resignation of Adam Sedgwick from his fellowship at Trinity College, Cambridge, in 1869, and the charge of heresy brought against Benjamin Jowett, Master of Balliol College, Oxford, in the same period. Interestingly enough, it was Jowett who worked hardest to secure government money for the new university colleges.

These shifts paved the way for the growth of anti-clericalism, ironically, especially in the ancient universities, during the middle decades of the twentieth century. Despite reform, both Oxford and Cambridge still continued to display many, at least, of the outward signs of a privileged status for the Church of England and the Christian religion. In Durham, Cambridge and Oxford Canon-Professorships in theology and Church history continued to exist.[15] In Oxbridge colleges there was, invariably, a chaplain, and often a Chaplain/Fellow. In Oxford, the cathedral served also as the chapel of the largest and best endowed of the colleges, Christ Church. Resistance to such privilege and scepticism in relation to the Christian faith was most sharply symbolized, one might argue, in the rise of logical positivism and the Vienna school of philosophy in the 1930s. A. J. Ayer's *Language, Truth and Logic* (1936) was in many ways the sacred text of this school of thought, arguing that talk of theology and ethics is meaningless, since they are impatient of verification. Although logical positivism enjoyed only a very brief ascendancy, nonetheless it was in this sceptical, anti-clerical and largely secularist atmosphere that the 'Robbins' or 'plate glass' (as they were then tabbed) universities were established in the early 1960s. The Robbins Report advocated the foundation of new universities in completely novel locations. These included East Anglia, Essex, Kent, Lancaster, Sussex, Warwick and York.

A brief glance at the foundation of one of these will paint the backdrop for cathedrals relating to universities in the later part of the twentieth century. East Anglia is a good choice, since it prided itself in being the most secular of all the new foundations, and there was some abrasive interaction between the academy, religion and the Church. This was well focused in a spat over the appointment of a Vice-Chancellor for the new university. Early on in the discussions, the Vice-Dean of Norwich Cathedral expressed an opinion: '[T]he new Vice-Chancellor should be "a man of wide sympathies and [with] an appreciation of the spiritual and cultural values that had contributed to our civilisation." Did he really mean "religious" values?

[asks the historian of the university].'[16] This concern about religion would cause more sparks as the appointment process moved on, and notably when Professor C. H. Waddington, a biologist and geneticist with wide cultural interests, but 'of doubtful Christianity', was suggested as prospective Vice-Chancellor. Waddington proved to have strange views on other topics but, although he was eventually offered the post, he then later turned it down. Along the way there were further bumps. One member of the founding Executive Committee asked about churchgoing. Launcelot Fleming, then Bishop of Norwich, a key player in the foundation of the university and former Cambridge don, who was very sensitive to the wider world beyond the Church, argued: 'No Test Act on V-C.'[17] The same man who had asked about churchgoing then made a still more pungent remark, saying that Waddington was 'not even a Christian'. This wounded Sir Solly Zuckerman (a very eminent government scientist and a member of the Academic Planning Board) who took the comment as an anti-Semitic slight. Ultimately, Bishop Fleming intervened again most emolliently by saying rather starkly now: 'Christian views irrelevant'.[18]

This perhaps unnecessarily exciting interlude gives a glimpse into the climate of the times. The bishop fought long and subtly to secure a space for a religious chaplaincy on the campus. The charter of the university still explicitly rules out confessional teaching, and is worded in such a manner that any form of theology department is still effectively ruled out of court. Ironically, Waddington, in his own eccentric way, had actually made clear his desire to establish 'a faculty of theology with initial instruction in divinity'.[19] Following this encounter, a fairly self-conscious feeling of secularity prevailed in the university, certainly for 25 years, and is still there in some quarters. The story, both in Norwich and throughout England, has, however, moved on. This leads us directly into a description and discussion of the opportunities available from profitable partnerships between cathedrals and universities at the present time.

Both Oxford and Durham retain the now unique office of Canon-Professorships. These combine directly a Residentiary Canonry at the cathedral with a professorship at the university. They offer particular possibilities, and can be seen as the tip of an iceberg where much more cooperation and linkage goes on underwater, so to speak, in the teaching of theology. The institutional links here also offer opportunities for interdisciplinary work which may or may not use the cathedral as the focus for such activity. In both these universities, as also in Cambridge, there is integrated cooperation between the university and various theological training institutions over the education of candidates for ordination. In Oxford, for example, the university validates both a BTh and an MTh, which are tailored to these purposes. Something of the historic links thus remain in these three places, albeit now painted imaginatively upon an ecumenical canvas.

Other cathedrals have developed rather different links, often with the cathedral initially making overtures to the university. So Chelmsford Cathedral developed good links with the University of Essex, leading to an institute for theological study offering courses at different levels, and in varied areas of specialism. In Manchester there has long been cooperation with the university, which helped establish a healthy extramural department, offering courses in applied theology. There is now no formal connection, but in the past a cathedral canonry was used to anchor these links. In Norwich, a strong partnership between the cathedral and the University of East Anglia has developed over a period covering the office of three successive vice-chancellors. The partnership has included three key components. There is a series of four annual lectures in honour of Bishop Launcelot Fleming, taking issues of broad social interest and including a theological twist; the first four sets of lectures have been published. The second strand has been a series of seminars on critical ethical issues, with the cathedral acting in concert with the appropriate university departments. Finally, 'a cathedral institute' has been established which, hopefully, will eventually deliver university-validated courses in areas of applied theology and associated subjects. At the Millennium there was also a conference on social conflict and social exclusion. This work is cemented by an annual meeting between the chapter and key members of the university's senior management team, headed by the vice-chancellor.

One of the most remarkable examples of university/cathedral partnership and collaboration is in Liverpool. In the mid-1980s, the cathedral chapter worked with John Moores University to regenerate the area immediately alongside the south side of the cathedral. There, within this development, are rented lodgings for 400 students of the university, together with buildings housing the university's media and critical arts department. The cathedral supported the establishment of the Foundation for Citizenship; this provides five public lectures each year on current social issues. Most recently of all, Lincoln Cathedral has launched a new School of Theology in partnership with the diocese of Lincoln, the University of Lincoln, Bishop Grosseteste College and the East Midlands Ministerial Training Course. The Lincoln School of Theology will offer part-time courses leading to a range of diplomas and degrees, as well as ministerial training. The university also intends to develop a postgraduate programme of professional development.[20] In Canterbury, strong links with the University of Kent exist, including the foundation of the Michael Ramsey Chair of Modern Theology. The current holder of that Professorship is also an honorary canon of Canterbury Cathedral. At St Albans, there are links between the cathedral and the universities of Hertfordshire and Cambridge, through the Ecumenical Christian Study Centre. Wakefield is at present looking into future cooperation with Leeds Metropolitan University. Portsmouth Cathedral has had long-standing links with the university in that city. University–cathedral links embrace all sorts of university foundations, and not only the ancient and redbrick institutions.

Further case studies confirm that where there is both a cathedral and a university in close proximity, the tendency is towards growth in collaboration. These university–cathedral links represent a significant contribution to further and higher education. Often they are underpinned by important personal interrelationships between university academics and those responsible for the theological development of cathedrals. Why this fairly significant shift in relationship in contrast to the rather more suspicious, even hostile, attitudes of the mid- and later twentieth century? The cynic would reply by saying that now 'everyone needs friends, and partnership is the slogan of the day'! There is some truth in this reflection. In recent years, universities have been exposed to market forces in a manner unknown in the past. Any partnership that might lead to a strengthening of numbers on specific courses ought to be pursued – hence cooperation on theological training.

Further, there has been, over the past 20 years, what some have described as the 'sad decline of serious atheism'. Despite the dogmatic assertions by Richard Dawkins, opposition to religion has become muted. At the time of writing, a trusted proponent of atheism, Anthony Flew, has just announced a change of mind, opting for a vague form of deism. Elsewhere, the cynics would say that there has been a great advancement in energetic apathy.

This, however, is to miss some real and positive developments. Cathedrals have begun to embrace more enthusiastically a role which has its roots deep in medieval culture. They do so, however, not for archaic reasons, but to play a fuller part in the increasing provision of education in a society which requires sophisticated and varied agencies of learning and teaching. Universities, too, when they are not being pursued by the rigours of research assessments, are now much more keen to enter the public arena and to work with other institutions to offer a broader educational model. Both universities and cathedrals, in different ways, help carry the spirit of the communities in which they are based. Imaginative cooperation between the two can issue in unexpected results. The establishment of the Sainsbury Institute for the Study of Japanese Arts and Cultures in the Close at Norwich is just one such initiative, arising almost by serendipity. There is, however, also an interesting intellectual convergence which may underlie this recent rapprochement between universities and cathedrals. There have been some seminal shifts in philosophical thought. It has not simply been a decline in serious atheism, but also a positive change in the mood of intellectual reflection. This has meant that even where scholars have remained agnostic they have engaged in intellectual reflection, which assumes an objectivity denying the prevalent relativism implied by so-called postmodernism. This has metaphysical implications, suggesting a rediscovered common ground between cathedrals and universities, religion and public life.

The publication of Alasdair MacIntyre's *After Virtue* was groundbreaking in its analysis of moral theory within the Western philosophical tradition.[21] The fact that it marked a movement full circle for MacIntyre back into the realms of belief is intriguing in itself. When one adds to this his recovery of the fundamental core of the Aristotelian tradition, and his plea for 'another – doubtless very different – St Benedict', then clearly there is both a remarkable shift and a convergence. This shift is not confined to MacIntyre, although, undoubtedly, his book has been very influential. Alongside MacIntyre, there has been published much interesting work which shows convergence of objective philosophical writing, tending towards theism. Two specific sets of essays are particularly interesting, issuing from highly contrasting backgrounds: the first set from the Dominican, Fergus Kerr OP, and the second from Stanley Hauerwas, the radical Methodist American moralist. They are both remarkable for their eclecticism.

Fergus Kerr, coming from a Thomist stable, explores writers as widely varied as Martha Nussbaum and Iris Murdoch. In a monograph which collects together his Stanton Lectures,[22] there is an analysis of the writings of not only the above two authors but also of Martin Heidegger, Luce Irigaray, Stanley Cavell, Charles Taylor and Karl Barth. Kerr's conclusion is that, despite the secular nature of some of these writings, still religious themes and an underlying exploration of meaning are resonant among these authors. In his preface, Kerr writes: 'Uncovering the theological connections at work in the projects of these philosophers, as well as sometimes clarifying what they are up to, often reveals the inadequacy of their assumptions about theology – Christian theology in all these cases.'[23] It is not only an 'Aunt Sally view of Christian theology' that Kerr discovers, however, but also a real tendency toward theological exploration, even where authors would explicitly rule themselves out as believers.

In his concluding chapter, Kerr is realistic about the impossibility of somehow seeking a 'grand initiative' which incorporates what he calls 'the traces and configurations of Christian theology . . . uncovered in some recent philosophical projects'.[24] Instead, Kerr moves on to talk of seven versions of transcending humanity. Kerr's final two sentences are tantalizing and encouraging, and may offer one pointer as to why cathedrals and universities have been able to be less defensive with each other and have even learned to collaborate. He writes:

77

> We do not have to choose between the leap in the dark of radical tran-
> scendence and hiding in the pure immanence of the familiar world.
> That is perhaps a theologian's dilemma that a philosopher of religion
> would hope to set aside.[25]

Perhaps dialogue between these two groups of people can be facilitated by a real encounter between cathedrals and the academy. In
contrast to the support of Kerr, what might Hauerwas have to offer?
His approach is utterly different, characteristically more aggressive
and combative to those both within and outside the Christian community. He is very keen that the Christian community should set a
challenge to the academy. Church is not to be subservient or insecure
in the face of university. So, Hauerwas begins thus:

> Theology is best done without apology. I therefore have no intention
> of apologising for the unapologetic character of this book. That I
> refuse to offer such an apology puts me at odds with a great deal of
> modern theology, which has adopted as its task to 'explain' – either to
> our cultural despisers or to what is a growing and more characteristic
> population, the indifferent – what Christians believe.[26]

This means that, as always, Hauerwas is keen to engage sharply with
Christian theologians. He also, however, interrogates non-believers in
a manner that bears fruit. Notable among these are, again, Martha
Nussbaum and Iris Murdoch.

Hauerwas is particularly bothered here to understand and criticize
Nussbaum's reading of Aristotle. It is clear that he is grateful for her
analysis, although at the end he makes no bones about his divergence
from her conclusions:

> [H]er attempt to recover a sense of the unavoidability of the con-
> tingent for a life of excellence as a free-standing truth can be seen as
> very profound advice for tired liberals who no longer believe in the
> Enlightenment project, but who know that they are condemned to live
> it out.[27]

Good knockabout stuff, but revealing about Hauerwas too. Hauerwas
is clear that the Nussbaum analysis comes near enough to the work of
Christian philosophers (like MacIntyre) for it to be important for him
to distance himself from her ultimate conclusions.

Similarly, in his argument with Iris Murdoch. So he notes early on in the essay: 'Of course a Christian theologian can use an atheist – particularly one as subtle as Miss Murdoch.'[28] In a footnote, Hauerwas notes the ambiguities of words like theism and atheism in a discussion of this sort. Indeed, in this case, his aim is to explore why Murdoch argues that we can no longer believe in the Christian God and he does so precisely to test how far Christian theologians may borrow her profound insights. His conclusion is that, as Christians, we have lost the appropriate depth of belief in our own convictions and tradition to engage in an effective argument. He reflects not only on her pure philosophy, but also on her imaginative writings: 'Even more than her philosophy, her novels present a temptation to Christians because inasmuch as we allow ourselves to be trained through them, we lose our ability to imagine another world.'[29] Hauerwas's argument doubtless contains more than a grain of truth. If this is so, where better to rediscover this other world than in the life and liturgy of cathedrals where the Christian story is dramatized and represented daily? Academy and Church desperately need each other; Athens and Jerusalem should not be held apart.

This brief excursion into recent debate between theologians and philosophers will come for some in the churches as a fascinating but, nevertheless, encouraging surprise; it reflects new possibilities for fostering an intellectual and educational partnership between the Church and the academy. It can help underpin the remarriage of religion and learning which has begun to develop within our cathedrals and universities. Perhaps the most regrettable thing about the twentieth century stand-off between the academy and the Church was its effect in neutralizing or denying real conversation between theologians and people of other disciplines, between those who count themselves as part of the believing community and those who could not so commit themselves. This new rapprochement is, indeed, happening at the same time as the demise of departments of theology in a number of universities. But perhaps the placing alongside universities of the worshipping tradition of cathedrals, together with the scholarly elements in these great foundations, could begin to respond to Hauerwas's combative questions to both non-believers and Christian theologians? In about AD 200 Tertullian asked, 'What has Athens to do with

Jerusalem?' The implied answer is nothing. Yet, somehow, that will not do, and the question will not go away – any more than the question of God's existence will go away. It did not go away for Hardy. In his sixties he bemoaned the fate of the Catholic Modernists at the hands of Cardinal Merry del Val; in his late eighties those tantalizing mists over Christminster had not disappeared – still he made his way over the fields from his home at Max Gate to evensong at Stinsford Church. Still the questions of God and of faith would not go away.

Both questions still remain. They were raised, obliquely, by George Steiner in his stimulating essay, *Real Presences*. At the beginning he puts it thus:

> [R]ational men and women, particularly in the scientific and techno-logical realities of the West, still refer to God. That is why the postulate of the existence of God persists in so many unconsidered turns of phrase and allusion. No plausible reflection or belief underwrites His presence ... [This essay] proposes that any coherent understanding of what language is, and how language performs, that any coherent account of the capacity of human speech to communicate meaning and feeling is, in the final analysis, underwritten by the assumption of God's presence.[30]

Might the still tentative, but growing, conversations between cathedrals and universities be able to contribute more to exploring this proposition?

Notes

1 Thomas Hardy, *Jude the Obscure*, Greenwood Edition (London, Macmillan, 1965), p. 125.
2 Hardy, *Jude the Obscure*, p. 92.
3 Hardy, *Jude the Obscure*, p. 95.
4 Hardy, *Jude the Obscure*, p. 101.
5 Hardy, *Jude the Obscure*, p. 156.
6 See Stephen Platten, 'Hurrying Forward to Heaven', *Humanitas*, vol. 3, no. 1 (October 2001), pp. 3–19.
7 David Parry OSB (ed.), *Households of God: The Rule of St Benedict with Explanations for Monks and Lay People Today* (London, Darton, Longman and Todd, 1980), from the Prologue, p. 1.

8 Parry, *Households of God*, p. 4.

9 Parry, *Households of God*, pp. 130–1, C. 48.

10 So, for example, Umberto Eco, *The Name of the Rose* (London, Secker and Warburg, 1983).

11 Grace Jantzen, *Julian of Norwich* (London, Darton, Longman and Todd, 1987), p. 17.

12 C. E. Whiting, *The University of Durham, 1832–1932* (London, Sheldon Press, 1932), pp. 30 and 33. Durell wrote: 'It has occurred to us that it will be prudent if possible to ward off the blow, and that no plan is so likely to take as marking the public partakers of our income by annexing an establishment of enlarged education.'

13 See Stephen G. Platten, 'The Conflict over the Control of Elementary Education 1870–1902 and Its Effect upon the Life and Influence of the Church', *The British Journal of Educational Studies*, vol. XXIII, no. 3 (October 1975), pp. 276–302.

14 Cf. Owen Chadwick, *The Victorian Church* (London, A. & C. Black, 1970), vol. 2, p. 461.

15 In Durham and Oxford such professorships still exist.

16 Michael Sanderson, *The History of the University of East Anglia, Norwich* (London, Hambledon and London, 2002), p. 34.

17 Sanderson, *The History of the University of East Anglia*, p. 36.

18 Sanderson, *The History of the University of East Anglia*, pp. 36 and 37.

19 Sanderson, *The History of the University of East Anglia*, p. 38.

20 *Church Times* (24 December 2004).

21 Alasdair MacIntyre, *After Virtue* (London, Duckworth, 1981). For Benedict quotation, see p. 245.

22 Fergus Kerr, *Immortal Longings* (London, SPCK, 1997).

23 Kerr, *Immortal Longings*, p. vii.

24 Kerr, *Immortal Longings*, p. 159.

25 Kerr, *Immortal Longings*, p. 184.

26 Stanley Hauerwas, *Wilderness Wanderings* (Boulder and Oxford, Westview Press, 1997), p. 1.

27 Hauerwas, *Wilderness Wanderings*, p. 93.

28 Hauerwas, *Wilderness Wanderings*, p. 156.

29 Hauerwas, *Wilderness Wanderings*, p. 167.

30 George Steiner, *Real Presences* (London, Faber, 1989), p. 3.

7

Cathedrals and urban life

MICHAEL SADGROVE

—◆—

Introduction: size isn't everything

The 'classic' perspective of an English cathedral is well summed up by Jonathan Glancey.

> Clearly, history has shown that we know how to create St John the Divine's 'heavenly city'. There are few buildings in Europe more beautiful or innovative than Ely Cathedral. This truly is one of those buildings that connects heaven to earth and reminds us that we're more than numbers, statistics and units . . . Our history also tells us that we know how to build small towns, where wonderful buildings rise up above vernacular rooftops: it all goes together, a wonderful little huddle.[1]

In these much-visited places, the relationship between city and cathedral is understood. There is in visual terms a respect for the way in which city and cathedral have evolved together, and represented a common vision of human life. Perhaps we can speak of a 'cathedral of the mind' that attaches to the image these cathedrals suggest, epitomized in Batsford books with their sepia mid-century photographs of a gentler and greener land. This imagined cathedral, a splendid medieval pile set in a close within a sleepy rural city, is deep rooted in the English folk-memory. It has its epiphanies in such places as Salisbury, Canterbury, Durham, Wells and Ely.

Sheffield, however, is on no-one's list of Britain's top architectural attractions, either ecclesiastical or civic. Of the city, Sir Nikolaus Pevsner wrote in 1959 with some asperity that 'architecturally, Sheffield is a miserable disappointment'.[2] Things have slowly improved. But it was telling that, when I was appointed Provost of Sheffield in 1995, a number of people tempered their good wishes by adding that they didn't know that Sheffield even *had* a cathedral. When I explained they said, 'Oh, not a real cathedral then.'[3]

Sheffield belongs to a group of cathedrals that deserves to be studied in greater depth, for the urban parish church cathedrals are half hidden and only half acknowledged at the heart of many of our cities. My reason for singling out this group is that we need to understand the problems and opportunities they face, often in highly strategic places and to people and institutions that drive regional if not national economies. I shall first say something about how parish church cathedrals came to be, then look at aspects of their life and mission, and finally suggest issues the wider Church needs to face in relation to them. In this, I shall use Sheffield Cathedral as a case study for, as both building and institution, it epitomizes many of the possibilities and problems encountered in the metamorphosis of a former parish church into a cathedral

The origins of parish church cathedrals

The urban parish church cathedrals are found in Birmingham, Blackburn, Bradford, Chelmsford, Coventry, Derby, Leicester, Manchester, Newcastle, Portsmouth, Sheffield, Southwark and Wakefield. These cathedrals rarely make the headlines, yet the importance of their locations is hard to overrate: they include a number of the 'core cities' of England recognized for their national economic significance. 'Parish church' cathedrals are parish churches that have been assigned the role of cathedral at a later stage in their history as a result of the creation of a new diocese. Legally, they remain parish churches. Their origin lay in the rapid expansion of many nineteenth- and twentieth-century cities through industrialization that resulted in the creation of new dioceses. Manchester, for example, was founded in 1847, Newcastle in 1882, Wakefield in 1888, and Birmingham and Southwark in 1905. Others were to follow in the next two decades.

Sheffield's fortunate position on the edge of the Pennines had always favoured manufacturing. Swift-running water, millstone grit and nearby coalfields had made for ideal conditions for the development of the cutlery industry. In the nineteenth century, Sheffield became renowned as the centre of steel manufacture in England. Its growth was staggering. In 1801, the population numbered around 31,000; in 1851, over 135,000; and in 1900 over 400,000.[4] In 1893, Sheffield became a city and by 1897 had its new town hall, crowned with the figure of Vulcan, a fitting monument to *fin de siècle* civic pride. The university was founded in 1905. The transformation of a remote Yorkshire town into a power house of British industry was complete.

At one level, the history of Sheffield Cathedral was part of the same movement towards establishing a new civic identity: a new city 'needed' a cathedral just as it needed a university and a town hall. By 1907 a bishopric committee had been established to promote the formation of a new diocese. An early, contentious, issue concerned the location of the cathedral, for 'the new See Town [of Sheffield] was not particularly happy in buildings suitable for its new status. The parish church, though large and venerable, was inconveniently arranged and lacked splendour, and was poor in "backstage" accommodation.'[5] 'T'owd church' of St Peter and St Paul was a typical Yorkshire Pennine church of blackened millstone grit, whose tower, spire and eastward portion was late medieval. Well loved, and with an enviable position, it was *as a building* scarcely adequate for the bishop's vision of a 'central spiritual force' for the diocese, a focus for 'wise and helpful experiments in our church life'.

What was meant by saying that the old parish church was 'inadequate for a cathedral' as the Cathedrals Commission of 1927 was to claim?[6] There is a lack of definition here. Theologically, to be a 'cathedral' means only one thing: to house the *cathedra*, the bishop's seat. Physical size does not enter into what a cathedral is *for*. This was never clearly articulated at that time. The presumption was that a cathedral's function was to be the gathering place of the diocese, and therefore *big*. This single issue dominated cathedral affairs from 1914, when the Diocese and Cathedral were founded, to 1966. Unlike at Leicester and Liverpool where there was talk of building a cathedral on a new site, the Commissioners of 1927 supported the view that the parish church 'should be wholly or in large measure rebuilt upon the present extensive site' but doubted whether it would be possible to incorporate most of the old church in the new building. This too was an important point.[7]

An influential book written during this period was F. S. M. Bennett's *The Nature of a Cathedral*. Bennett was Dean of Chester. His section on 'New Dioceses and Their Cathedrals' puts the Sheffield debate into an illuminating context. New dioceses, he says, should think *de novo* about what they want from their cathedrals, but he states as an axiom that 'an old parish church should never never never [*sic*] be chosen for this purpose'. Not only are parish churches inadequate as buildings: there is a fundamental difference between the nature of a cathedral and a parish church.

> A cathedral is not merely a parish church on a huge scale. It is the Family House of God of a diocese, which is quite a different thing . . . A cathedral must keep itself diocesan. It will always be tempted to become too parochial in its city and its city will always love to have it so.[8]

Moreover, the bishop should live nearby so that he and his *familia* can pray together; the diocesan offices should be part of its close, and it should include sufficient space for hospitality to parish clergy. Of the modern cathedrals, Liverpool is his ideal. But then he waxes eloquent about 'fortunate Chester', which he calls, revealingly, 'a great ecclesiastical Town Hall, on a scale that many a municipality might covet'.

The Cathedral Enlargement Committee met in 1921 and engaged as architect Charles Nicholson, a baronet formed in the neo-Gothic tradition influenced by the Arts and Crafts movement. His first foray into the cathedral world was to submit an unsuccessful design for the Liverpool Cathedral competition in 1902. The spate of new dioceses created between the 1880s and the late 1920s offered him plenty of scope. Nicholson was architect to no less than four of the new cathedrals: Chelmsford and Sheffield (both 1914), Bradford (1919) and Portsmouth (1927).[9] It was his misfortune that none of his schemes for the enlargement of parish church cathedrals was ever completed.

Nicholson's initial advice to his four 'new' cathedrals was the same: build on to the north, incorporating the medieval fabric into the larger building. At Sheffield, Nicholson's plan was the same as at Chelmsford and Bradford: to make the existing nave the south aisle of a new nave laid alongside it to the north. (This had already been done at Truro Cathedral in Nicholson's native West Country, where St Mary's Aisle, incorporated into Pearson's majestic building on the south side, is still legally a parish church.) His Sheffield Cathedral would have been a wide-bodied church seating 3,000 people. The per-petuated parish-church-as-south aisle tells us what Nicholson then believed about parish church cathedrals: that the memory of their parochial identity needed to be clearly preserved.

In the aftermath of war, costs proved prohibitive and the plans were shelved. In 1932 Alfred Jarvis became Vicar of Sheffield and its first Provost. A former Chaplain-General of the Forces, he set about the transformation of the cathedral with military energy, perceiving that the church was at risk of becoming, in his words, 'a mausoleum or a convalescent depot'. A great church was certainly his vision: 'we need a cathedral, not an adapted parish church'. By now Nicholson had thought again. He decided to rotate the axis by 90 degrees with a longer nave running north to south across the existing one, the medieval sanctuary becoming a 'south' transept, with a second tower and spire marking a new 'north' transept. Significantly, it was as if Nicholson was abandoning his belief that an enlarged parish church cathedral had to preserve as much as possible of the original parish church. The new scheme made no pretence at piety towards the old church; indeed, it ran right across it in a way that absorbed its old identity. This seems to symbolize the recognition that, under the new system of governance being introduced at precisely this time, the cathedral was taking a new direction, its parochial life being sub-sumed into a larger cathedral role.

The building of Nicholson's 'grandiose and revolutionary' cathe-dral[10] began in 1937. Work proceeded rapidly. In 1939 the Chapter House, vestries and St George's Chapel were consecrated and there-after the construction of the other liturgical spaces on the north side proceeded according to plan. But it is one of the cathedral's most quoted stories that the nave failed to be built by just one day. Work was due to begin above ground on Monday 4 September 1939. War was declared on the Sunday. It was not an auspicious date to embark on so big an undertaking. Jarvis was not to know that, when work on the new nave stopped that day, it would be for ever.

After the war, the will to complete the cathedral began to falter for lack of resource, though funds were already inadequate in 1939. Nicholson's final building, the Holy Spirit Chapel, was finished in 1948. After that, Provost Jarvis retired, and in 1949 Nicholson died. He was followed by Stephen Dykes Bower, and then George Pace who completely redrew Nicholson's scheme. He wrote in 1957:

> There is now a much wider understanding of the basis of modern architecture in the service of the church, and with that understanding a desire that the nave and quire of the new cathedral shall be a theological affirmation, expressed in the living architecture of this century.

He acknowledged that he must 'pay proper homage to the ancient portions ... [and] respect the great axis laid down by Sir Charles Nicholson ... But within this framework, something tremendous is possible.'[11]

Pace's nave also ran north–south, seating 800 people. He envisaged the quire as doing duty also as the parish church, a reversion to the earlier Nicholson philosophy. The liturgical north wall was conceived as a monumental continuous window along the lines of Le Corbusier's Chapel at Ronchamps. But again it was cost that was to prove decisive. For the third and last time, a proposed cathedral was never built. In 1961, the council abandoned for good schemes to build on the north–south axis and wrote a new more modest brief that reverted to the medieval orientation. Pace resigned, invoking the 40-year-old mantra that this would merely 'produce a larger parish church, never a cathedral'. Arthur Bailey succeeded him and, in 1966, completed the present west-end extension which merely involved pulling down the west wall to extend the nave by 28 feet.

I have told this story in detail because it illustrates the problems and paradoxes inherent in the wish to adapt a town church to the role of cathedral. The endless discussions and aborted plans of half a century were not solely about rebuilding or reordering a church. They acted out the struggle of a parish church to make sense of its new status and role of 'cathedral'. Such a story can be told many times over in urban parish church cathedrals. We shall return towards the end of this essay to the question of what this might mean for parish church cathedrals in a new century.

The mission of parish church cathedrals

The emergence of parish church cathedrals in the nineteenth and twentieth centuries looks at first sight like a unique episode in the history of English cathedrals. But there are intriguing parallels with the history of another group of cathedrals, and to recognize this may help place our discussion in a larger context.

When I came to Durham I did not expect much of my Sheffield experience to be transferable to a cathedral so different from it. However, one aspect of Durham's history felt familiar. Like Sheffield, it too had undergone a change of role in the past. The dormitory, refectory, monks' kitchen, even the prior's lodging in which I now lived, testified to the turbulent journey made during the sixteenth century from monastic cathedral priory to secular foundation. The analogy seemed to be that here were two cathedrals that had both been required to relearn their role in a new world that required a very different approach to mission. Just as Durham had needed to relinquish its monastic past and acquire the identity of a secular cathedral, so Sheffield had needed to leave its parochial past behind if it was to prove equal to the challenge of its newly acquired cathedral identity.

The importance of these questions for Sheffield is illustrated by how the governance of that cathedral has evolved. For the first 20 years of its life, like the other parish church cathedrals, it remained wholly parochial. Its incumbent was known as the 'Vicar of Sheffield', his colleagues were curates, and its cathedral role was in effect 'bolted on' to its existing parochial functions. The Cathedrals Commission of 1927 had much to say about this. It adopted a lengthy statement on aims that it believed applied to all cathedrals, irrespective of history, context or location. It affirmed that each cathedral is

> the place of the bishop's seat, the mother church of the diocese . . . maintained by the corporate religious life of the deans and canons and other officers . . . the home and school of religious art – architecture, craftsmanship and music – and of religious learning.[12]

It recognized that cathedrals had 'great functions in the life of the Church and Nation'.

The parish church cathedrals were given careful consideration. Their position was 'in many ways anomalous and confused'[13] because of the haphazard and individual way their organizations had evolved. It proposed a unified system of governance that recognized the distinctiveness of parish church cathedrals. It called for an entirely new governing body of clergy and laity to be called the Cathedral Council, and for the incumbent to be styled 'Provost', a conscious avoidance of the title 'Dean' with its medieval associations. The bishop would retain the jurisdiction he already enjoyed as ordinary of the parish church, and its patronage would be vested in him if it were not his already (an issue at Sheffield and Bradford, whose patrons were private trustees).

New constitutions and statutes for parish church cathedrals came into force under the Cathedrals Measure of 1931. The Commission had recognized the importance of clarifying the relationship between the two roles of cathedral and parish church. They were careful to distinguish, as a governance issue, what belonged to one and what to the other. The new structure of Provost and Council was applicable only to the cathedral aspect of the church's life. Its parochial ministry would continue much as before, and the Parochial Church Council would continue to administer it. The Commission recognized that this was perhaps a transitional arrangement. Some members believed that, ultimately, either these churches should be freed from their parish connections altogether, or wholly new cathedrals should be built, as at Liverpool. But it was agreed that 'a fully constituted chapter on the basis of the older cathedrals should not be set up to govern any cathedral church unless or until it is relieved from its parochial conditions'.[14]

As we have seen, it was precisely at this time that Sheffield Cathedral symbolically proceeded to give architectural expression to its newly acquired identity. But thinking about the true *nature* of a parish church cathedral remained confused. As the historical note at the conclusion of the 1994 report of the Howe Commission on Cathedrals, *Heritage and Renewal*, noted, 'it was surprising that the establishment of the parish church cathedrals did not stimulate thought about the functions of cathedrals generally'.[15] At Sheffield, Bishop Leslie Hunter wrote in 1954 in a striking echo of Bennett:

In these Parish Church Cathedrals, the use and usefulness of the Church as a Parish Church must always be the first consideration. To do anything to limit the use and usefulness of the old Parish Church of a great City would be wrong . . . Any modifications or additions to the building which might make it more suitable for diocesan purposes . . . have to be considered *in the light of the primary and continuing purpose of the Parish Church*. Parish Churches, with their local, historical associations and intimate uses, cannot be converted into Cathedrals 'on the grand scale' together with the kind of collegiate worship maintained by a residentiary chapter, without losing their character and traditional purpose. If a Diocese desires and can afford a Cathedral of that sort, it should be built on a new and unrestricted site.[16]

Heritage and Renewal recommended that the distinction between 'parish church' and 'dean and chapter' cathedrals should be abolished. It did this on the basis of a clearly articulated theological assumption, that cathedrals existed to serve 'the organisation of the mission of the Church in the world . . . The cathedral . . . is "the seat of the bishop and a centre of worship and mission".'[17] Officially, 'parish church cathedrals' do not exist, any more than 'dean and chapter' cathedrals. There are only *cathedrals*, governed by chapters presided over by deans, answerable to councils. And while questions may be asked about whether this definition was the best that could be achieved, it did at least identify that the primary task of a parish church cathedral was to be a diocesan cathedral. This is clearly progress, although, as I shall argue later, it still leaves certain questions unresolved.

I arrived at Sheffield in 1995, the year following the publication of the Commission's report. I was pleased to find a cathedral vigorously pursuing a creative mission at the heart of one of England's great industrial cities. There was a loyal, committed community of worshippers and a high standard of liturgy and music. There were fruitful relationships with the community of South Yorkshire and the city's leadership and strong links with arts and education. The regeneration of the city was reflected in an ambitious vision for the cathedral's development, the first-fruits of which was the reconstruction of the cathedral forecourt to signal a sense of connection between the cathedral and the city centre. Most impressive of all was the cathedral's work among homeless and disadvantaged people, its Breakfast Project that provided a cooked meal five mornings a week to upwards of 50 or 60 needy and deprived people, and the Archer Project, a drop-in centre offering to the same constituency an array of social, educational, cultural and recreational facilities and comprehensive personal support. As an instance of the Church engaging with urban poverty, it was (and is) a model of professionalism and excellence.

But much of this good work could and would have been pursued by any adequately resourced city-centre church. Cities like Sunderland, Southampton, Leeds and Nottingham come to mind as places with lively city-centre churches offering similar ministries but with no cathedral. I found myself asking what difference to the mission of Sheffield Parish Church being 'cathedral' actually made. (It is true that cathedrals attract significant funding from the Church Commissioners, not available to parishes: the stipends of the dean and two canons, and – apart from the less impoverished cathedrals – a block grant.)

However, it seemed to me that the core question of *aims* had still not been addressed, despite the Cathedrals Measure. This was tellingly expressed in the cathedral's pattern of worship. I found that the Eucharist was celebrated no less than three times on a Sunday morning, with an early morning Prayer Book service and two later celebrations. The second, at 9.30 a.m., was called the Parish Communion; the third, at 11 a.m., the Cathedral Eucharist. This later service was an eastward-facing celebration at the high altar in traditional language, fully choral with no lay participation in the reading of lessons or prayers. The earlier service was a westward-facing celebration at a nave altar in contemporary language with hymns but no choir, a congregational act of worship with much lay involvement. It was followed by a parish breakfast.

There seemed to me to be an anomaly here. The earlier congregation looked for 'parish' worship: contemporary, informal, intimate. The later one looked for 'cathedral' liturgy: traditional, choral, transcendent. There seemed to be no meeting point between these two liturgical cultures. And, while each had its strengths, each seemed also to play into the fantasies the other group had about it. To the 'parish' congregation, the 'cathedral' service was distant, remote, non-participative and elitist, while to the 'cathedral' people, the earlier service was casual, lacking atmosphere and without reverence. To me, this acting out within a single institution of a 'cathedral' culture and a 'parish' culture was symbolic of a flawed ecclesiology. But it was true to the systemic arrangement at the heart of the cathedral's governance which included not only a Cathedral Council but also a Parochial Church Council, another example of old, unresolved issues.

This raised sharply for me the question of *aims* and *meanings* in an ecclesial community, and how this should be expressed in worship and common life. It is not coincidence that at about this time we set to writing a mission statement for the cathedral. A group of lay people agreed to hammer out what they considered to be the core aims of the cathedral and submit this to the Council for formal endorsement. As an exercise, it could not have been bettered as a way of reflecting on the purpose of an urban cathedral. It affirmed that the Cathedral is both the seat of the Bishop of Sheffield and 'an ancient part of the city's heritage, and a place of ceremony, pilgrimage, sanctuary and meeting . . . a place of prayer [and] . . . a resource for the churches and people of the region'. In due course, the 'two-tier' Sunday morning worship was abandoned in favour of a single act of worship known as 'the Sung Eucharist'. This was not simply a merger of its two predecessors, but an altogether new rite worked out from first principles that posed the question, how can the central liturgical action of the week best express the cathedral's purpose and aims? Our answer was a modern-language liturgy celebrated westwards at the *high* altar (rather than in the nave), fully choral but with much lay participation.

In 2000, Sheffield was one of the first cathedrals to implement the Cathedrals Measure, whereby the former Cathedral Council and the Parochial Church Council were both abolished, and a single set of cathedral-focused instruments put in their place.

Parish church cathedrals in the twenty-first century

At Sheffield I believed that unless this parish church cathedral embraced its proper vocation with conviction and organized its mission in the light of it, it would forever limp between the two opinions of whether it was a 'real' cathedral or simply a large parish church. In this, I was perhaps singing to a different tune from that of the first Bishop of Sheffield with whom I worked, David Lunn. In his witty and learned history of the cathedral, he indulged in a 'partisan post-script' in which he expressed his misgivings about the way the parish church had been forced into the procrustean bed of a cathedral. Of the 1931 Measure he asks why cathedrals should all be treated in the same way.

> There was [he thinks] an ideal Cathedral laid up in heaven and all Cathedrals were to be as close to that ideal as possible. But that ideal Cathedral was astonishingly like an old Cathedral of England. And great and continuing harm is done by the attempt to live out the word 'Cathedral' as though it had to mean Lincoln, York or Ely![18]

During the 1990s, a similar debate was taking place in the world of higher education around the proposal that the former polytechnics should become fully fledged degree-awarding universities, with their principals becoming vice-chancellors. A handful of principals at first resisted this metamorphosis on the grounds that this would send out a misleading message about the true nature of their institutions. Historically, they argued, polytechnics did not set out to emulate universities but represented a *sui generis* vocationally-orientated education that was distinct from university provision and therefore able to complement it. They did not wish to join the 'older' universities as 'poor relations'. This 'purist' approach did not find favour among the majority, and polytechnics are now a matter of history.

This analogy strikes me even more forcibly now that I reflect on it from the standpoint of a deanery in a medieval cathedral. Are Sheffield and Durham different only in scale and history, or also in vocation? The unfinished business in the evolution of parish church cathedrals leaves this question unanswered, whatever the theory may say. So I shall conclude by suggesting a number of issues that the whole Church needs to face if parish church cathedrals are to be as effective as the new universities in 'coming of age'.

First, it is vital that the parish church cathedrals are properly resourced for the tasks Church and society increasingly ask and expect of them. Unlike the historic cathedrals, the vast majority of parish church cathedrals have next to no historic endowments, and their financial position is precarious to say the least. What is more, their capacity to generate new income streams is severely limited by their largely not being buildings of national importance situated on the main tourist routes and attracting large numbers of visitors. The financial support of the Church Commissioners through stipend payments and block grants is vital to their task, as is government support for fabric maintenance through English Heritage grant aid. But it is not enough. Given the success of these cathedrals in engaging seriously and creatively with the urban agenda, it is vital that more central resources are put their way through the augmentation of grants and the reinstatement of support for the maintenance of their clergy houses. It is asking for bricks to be made of straw to expect them even to survive under such a harsh economic regime, let alone think that they might prosper.

Second, bishops and dioceses with parish church cathedrals need to reflect on what they look for from their cathedrals. A traditional cathedral has the critical 'mass', and the confidence that comes from a long history, to evolve in its own way and, if it were so minded, develop ministries tangential or even antipathetic to those of the diocese. This can never be the case with a parish church cathedral. Its very viability, not to say flourishing, depends on the closest possible goodwill and synergy between bishop and chapter, diocese and cathedral. I learned in Sheffield how vital it is for both bishop and dean to establish confidence and trust in their relationship. The bishop needs to be a frequent participant in cathedral worship and activity; the dean needs to be a conscientious member of the bishop's staff meeting and player in the diocesan arena. This, of course, ought to be true of *all* bishops and deans, but I suggest that it is especially important in urban dioceses.

The Cathedrals Measure envisages and requires that bishops and chapters consult regularly about the mission of their cathedral. This partnership is fundamental to the task. But it is perhaps worth observing that some of the newer dioceses continue to be cautious about putting resources into their cathedrals, whether financial or in kind; on the contrary, many ill-funded parish church cathedrals pay a parish share to the diocese. To ask for practical commitment on the part of the diocese to its cathedral would be to take seriously the logic of its being 'the seat of the bishop'. A parish church cathedral is not, historically, the 'mother church' of its diocese (perhaps a phrase we could all usefully lose), but it is metaphorically its 'parish church', and this should be reflected both in a realistic funding relationship and in the active participation of the diocese in its governance and ministry.

Third, the issue of identity still remains unresolved. Despite the 1999 Measure, parish church cathedrals still continue to exist as an intriguing and problematic group. For one thing, *Heritage and Renewal* balked at tackling some of their more intractable issues. It did not recommend that parish church cathedrals should be taken out of the parish system once and for all as a sign of their having a new set of priorities quite different from their historical parochial roles. The statistics cited in the report[19] demonstrated that the majority of parish church cathedrals had negligible parochial populations. Sheffield's was given as 637. In the light of this it was anomalous that the existence of parish church cathedrals was consciously perpetuated into the twenty-first century.

A related matter concerned patronage. Deans of the ancient cathedrals are appointed by the Crown, those of parish church cathedrals mainly by the bishop or, at Bradford and Sheffield, by trustees. While *Heritage and Renewal* called for the appointment process to be as 'uniform as possible',[20] it did not recommend a unified system under which bishops should transfer their patronage to the Crown or vice-versa. Yet if the defence of the Crown's role in appointments to deaneries is valid, that is, that deans are office holders in the *national* church and not simply diocesan clergy, then it is valid for all deaneries. Similarly, if it is argued that a bishop ought to be free to appoint *all* the members of his staff in order to build an effective team, then this too applies in every case and not just in some. And the continued involvement of private trustees in appointments to two deaneries is surely anomalous.

All this puts a drag on the process of assimilation to a fully fledged cathedral role. It runs counter to the 'meaning' of cathedral as the legislation understands it. It confuses the true nature of a cathedral's mission, and prevents 'coming of age'. It is not surprising that the evolution of parish church cathedrals since the nineteenth century has been hesitant, muddled and beset by unclear aims and considerable self-doubt. It is time that this is put right. I am not pretending that it is easy to make the journey from parish congregation to cathedral community, any more than the transition from monastic cathedral priory to secular cathedral was straightforward in the sixteenth century. But just such a focus on diocesan-wide and city-wide ministry is needed in urban areas, and it is important that cathedral aims and constitutions reflect this.

Fourth, we need to return to the issue of buildings. It is impossible to generalize here. But I suggest that what cities need in their cathedrals is not primarily that they are necessarily able to accommodate great crowds of people (the medieval cathedrals were not built for this purpose either). It is rather to achieve in terms of spatial and aesthetic *quality* a sufficient sense of the numinous that can function symbolically as both sacred and public space in their own right. To use the language of Henri Lefebvre, it is to project into the 'near order' a symbol of the 'far order',[21] or, as theology puts it, a sign of transcendence that is 'not purely functional but evocative'.[22] At Liverpool and Coventry, opportunity arose to create such spaces anew in a way that could invest the 'temple' with the same presence and dignity as the city's peer institutions of academy, town hall, gymnasium and market place. The smaller parish church cathedrals are inevitably the result of compromises between vision and resource. This can often be read directly out of the architectural history of the buildings themselves, as the history of Sheffield shows.

It is not a question of whether they are capable *as buildings* of carrying the weight of spiritual, historical, cultural and civic meaning cities look to them for, but of how this is to be achieved. The development of Portsmouth Cathedral suggests how a modest space can speak of large things in a way that is convincing and even moving. It is indisputably a 'cathedral', that is, a church organized spatially around the presumption, not of a parish congregation seated for Sunday worship, but of an environment in which the people gather as in an *agora* to be taught by the bishop and led by him in the celebration of the liturgy. Again, the adaptation (usually, over several generations) of great monastic churches to their new role as secular cathedrals illustrates a process that needs more confidently to happen in parish church cathedrals if they are to rise to the welcome expectations being placed on them.

Finally, we should not forget the handful of large cities that did not acquire their own cathedrals. Usually, this is because of a large and ancient cathedral or greater church nearby. Leeds, Nottingham, Sunderland, Plymouth and Southampton come to mind. Such cities need a centrally placed, properly resourced Christian presence that will both provide sacred space at their heart and also minister to every dimension of city life. Recent years have seen the establishment of urban 'minsters', parish churches at which a city-wide ministry and mission is located in the context of daily prayer and common life, for example, Preston, Dewsbury, Doncaster, Rotherham and Sunderland. A recent report on Sunderland Minster tries to learn from the ambiguous history of parish church cathedrals and suggests ways in which its aims, identity and governance could free it of parochial constraints in order to deliver a more effective city-wide ministry. Parish church cathedrals, with their histories and expertise, are well placed to assist in the formation and development of these forms of church life that are likely to prove highly significant as focal points of mission in our cities.

Conclusion

The recent Church of England Report, *Mission-shaped Church*, is providing us with a language with which to speak about the Church's evangelistic and missionary engagement with the world. 'The changing nature of our missionary context requires a new inculturation of the gospel within our society.'[23] It recognizes that one of the key changes in UK society in recent decades has been its increasingly urban character. While the report had next to nothing to say about the innovative and imaginative ways in which cathedrals specifically have borne witness to Jesus Christ, it is right to point out that mission strategy in the new millennium will require new approaches that in turn both form and spring out of 'fresh expressions' of church life.

We have seen how the emergence of urban parish church cathedrals was an answer to the question of how the gospel was to be proclaimed at the heart of our nation's great cities. They were conceived as 'fresh expressions', new and at the time untested ways of configuring and inculturating Christian presence and community amid the possibilities and challenges posed by urbanization. I have argued that this experiment is still 'work in progress', and that it deserves to continue to be believed and invested in as part of the Church's continuing response to the imperatives of worship and mission in our cities. The vitality of many parish church cathedrals is impressive, even moving. But they face significant threats, both *philosophically* (how can their true purpose within a 'mission-shaped' Church be properly stated, understood and owned?) and *practically* (how can their mission be adequately resourced?). In addressing these fundamental questions, the next decade of their short but fascinating life is likely to prove crucial.

Notes

1 Jonathan Glancey, 'A New England?', *RSA Journal* (February 2005), p. 25 (abbreviated transcript of a lecture 'The Regeneration Game: What's Really Happening to Our Cities?', given to the Royal Society of Arts in October 2004; the full text is at <www.theRSA.org.events>).
2 Nikolaus Pevsner, *The Buildings of England: West Riding of Yorkshire*, 1st edn, 1959, cited in the 2nd edn revised by Enid Radcliffe (Harmondsworth, Penguin Books, 1967), p. 447.
3 This innocence is shared by a recent social-scientific study of Sheffield: Ian Taylor, Karne Evans and Penny Fraser, *A Tale of Two Cities: Global Change, Local Feeling and Everyday Life in the North of England: A Study in Manchester and Sheffield* (London, Routledge, 1996). In this illuminating and impressive survey, there is but a single (historical) reference to Manchester Cathedral, and none at all to Sheffield Cathedral.
4 For an account of the growth of Sheffield as a consequence of the Industrial Revolution, and its impact on the Parish Church, see E. R. Wickham, *Church and People in an Industrial City* (London, Lutterworth Press, 1957).
5 Mary Walton, *A History of the Diocese of Sheffield 1914–1979* (Sheffield, Sheffield Diocesan Board of Finance, 1981), p. 12.
6 Church Assembly, *Report of the Cathedrals Commission 1927* (London, Church Assembly, 1927), pp. 242ff. The delegation responsible for the report on Sheffield Cathedral was chaired by W. H. Frere, Bishop of Truro.
7 Church Assembly, *Report of the Cathedrals Commission 1927*, p. 245.
8 F. S. M. Bennett, *The Nature of a Cathedral* (Chester, Phillipson and Golder, and London, A. R. Mowbray, 1925), pp. 66–7.

9 On Nicholson's work at Portsmouth Cathedral, see Sarah Quail and Alan Wilkinson (eds), *Forever Building: Essays to Mark the Completion of the Cathedral Church of St. Thomas of Canterbury* (Portsmouth, Portsmouth Cathedral Council, 1995).

10 George Tolley, *We of Our Bounty: A History of the Sheffield Church Burgesses* (The Memoir Club, 1999), p. 54.

11 Peter Pace, *The Architecture of George Pace* (London, Batsford, 1990), p. 175, citing Pace's text in the official appeal brochure of 1957.

12 Church Assembly, *Report of the Cathedrals Commission 1927*, pp. 9–10.

13 Church Assembly, *Report of the Cathedrals Commission 1927*, pp. 21–2.

14 Church Assembly, *Report of the Cathedrals Commission 1927*, p. 22.

15 *Heritage and Renewal: The Report of the Archbishops' Commission on Cathedrals* (London, Church House Publishing, 1994), p. 195.

16 Quoted in David Lunn, *Chapters toward a History of the Cathedral and Parish Church of St Peter and St Paul Sheffield* (Sheffield, Bishop's Office, Diocese of Sheffield, 1987), pp. 23–4.

17 *Heritage and Renewal*, pp. 3–4.

18 Lunn, *Chapters toward a History of the Cathedral and Parish Church of St Peter and St Paul Sheffield*, p. 34.

19 Lunn, *Chapters toward a History of the Cathedral and Parish Church of St Peter and St Paul Sheffield*, p. 59.

20 Lunn, *Chapters toward a History of the Cathedral and Parish Church of St Peter and St Paul Sheffield*, p. 88.

21 Henri Lefebvre, *Writings on Cities*, translated and edited by Eleonore Kofman and Elizabeth Lebas (Oxford, Blackwell, 1996), p. 114.

22 Philip Sheldrake, *Spaces for the Sacred: Place, Memory and Identity* (London, SCM Press, 2001), p. 154.

23 *Mission-shaped Church: Church Planting and Fresh Expressions of Church in a Changing Context* (London, Church House Publishing, 2004) (a Church of England report), p. xii.

8

From the past to the future: Archaeology and the conservation of cathedrals

PHILIP THOMAS

———◆———

The archaeology of cathedrals

On 8 April 2005, away from public view, the body of Pope John Paul II was interred in the Vatican grottoes alongside the bodies of his predecessors and close to the shrine of the very first bishop of Rome, St Peter. In his last will and testament the Pope revealed that he had considered burial in his native Poland, but left the final decision to the College of Cardinals. Amid calls for his canonization, it is no surprise that the Vatican has secured his body for itself; another papal saint will further increase the sanctity of St Peter's Basilica. All this has a particular relevance to archaeology, as the Pope's resting place is beneath the current sixteenth-century basilica, within the foundations of what must be the earliest cathedral built, Old St Peter's. This was founded by the emperor Constantine c. AD 320–30.

But what of English cathedrals, what are their origins? Why are they where they are, and why are they as they are? Although a small number of English Roman sites, such as Lullingstone in Kent, have been interpreted as churches, we have yet to discover a Roman cathedral or Christian basilica in this country. They must have existed as both London and York are known to have had bishops from as early as the fourth century.[1] With the decline of the Roman Empire, however, there was a setback, as Christianity in Britain waned and was not rekindled until the sixth and seventh centuries when later missionaries arrived. In the latter century the papacy established dioceses in England, ruled over (as they are today) by the provinces of Canterbury and York. Each diocese had a bishop, and the church which held his throne was known as the cathedral. Now, probably for the first time there was a network of cathedrals created across the country. In terms of location, the pope was inclined to establish these early cathedrals in former Roman towns despite the fact many had since dwindled in size.[2] These earliest churches were modelled on Roman basilicas, but there may have also been some use of existing buildings. In his instructions to St Augustine, Pope Gregory ruled that:

> [I]dol temples of that race (the English) should by no means be destroyed, but only the idols in them . . . For if the shrines are well-built it is essential that they should be changed from the worship of devils to the service of the true God.[3]

This was a very pragmatic approach, and is comparable to the transfer of Christian feastdays to pagan festivals. One possible example of such continuity is at Wells, in Somerset; here a small, sunken, rectangular building was discovered during excavations in 1978. One interpretation of this is that it is a Roman mausoleum, the first in a series of buildings on the site which culminate in the present cathedral. If proved correct, this demonstrates at least 1,600 years of ritual continuity since Wells was a Roman cult site.[4]

One of the earliest Anglo-Saxon cathedrals was that of Rochester, founded in AD 604. This was excavated in the late nineteenth century and found to be north-west of the present church. Rochester is one of a number of early cathedrals whose foundation was recorded by the Venerable Bede in his *Ecclesiastical History* (AD 731). By the late Saxon period, dioceses had been established over most of England. Cathedrals were getting bigger; excavations have uncovered large buildings at Winchester and Canterbury; indeed repairing and the provision of underfloor heating in the early 1990s revealed the Saxon cathedral's foundations beneath the present nave at Canterbury. The (mostly) unexcavated foundations of Wells lie under the Gothic cloister. But it is not just excavation that provides evidence. Remarkably, some *standing* fabric still survives from Saxon cathedrals. The west wall of Sherborne Abbey dates to the time when this building was the centre of the diocese rather than Salisbury.[5] Likewise, part of the nave at Dorchester Abbey represents the cathedral of the see which later moved to Lincoln. Sometimes the evidence for earlier churches is the reuse of fabric; St Albans incorporates Anglo-Saxon shafts, and Worcester reuses Saxon capitals. The only evidence for the earliest church at Ely is a carved stone of *c.* 700–800 which was reused in the thirteenth-century Hospital of St John.[6]

Norman power demonstrated

Although some cathedrals can trace their roots back to the Saxon period, not all cathedral churches were originally founded as seats of bishops; some were founded as monasteries and became cathedrals at a later date. Henry VIII created six new cathedrals from monasteries after the Dissolution (Bristol, Chester, Gloucester, Oxford, Peterborough and Westminster Abbey). He also re-established the majority of monastic cathedrals as secular institutions, with canons replacing monks. This idea of monastic cathedrals dates to Saxon times and was unique to Britain. After the Conquest Archbishop Lanfranc made even more cathedrals monastic so in total half of the 18 cathedrals were run by monks.[7] This was not the only change under Lanfranc and the Normans. In 1071 the Archbishop began to rebuild his cathedral at Canterbury and during the next half century all other cathedrals were rebuilt in the new architecture of the ruling elite, Romanesque. In addition to rebuilding, some cathedrals were actually relocated. The king persuaded the Bishop of Wells to move his seat from the 'village' of Wells to the larger town of Bath, likewise Dorchester was moved to Lincoln, and the see of Norwich is thought to have originated at Elmham. Relocation was not a new idea, as Edward the Confessor had moved the cathedral for Devon from Crediton to Exeter back in 1050, but the scale of both the changes and the new buildings was unique, and a reflection of the power of the Norman king and his church.[8] In fact, the relocation of cathedrals was just one of a number of changes implemented by Lanfranc in the most radical church reform before the Reformation. William the Conqueror used the Church as a means to implement his rule, and the foundation of cathedrals in larger towns established a Norman power base especially when presided over by Norman clergy. So the king gave land of '14 dwellings' in Norwich to encourage the establishment of the cathedral and this was expanded on by Bishop Losinga in order to found his cathedral in 1096.

William I enforced his rule by building castles to accompany these new cathedrals. The ruins of Old Sarum show that a castle, palace and cathedral all occupied the small hill top, and not one but two castles were built close to Ely Cathedral.[9] In Norwich not only did the city have a castle, but also the bishop built his own keep connected to the north side of the cathedral. Norwich, Lincoln and many other cathedral cities were suddenly dominated by huge buildings which towered over their houses reinforcing Norman rule. Sometimes it was the bishops who enforced law themselves; Lanfranc put down the insurrection at Norwich Castle, and the Bishop of Durham was responsible for securing the Scottish border. The clergy were clearly tools of the Crown. Not only did these finished buildings dominate settlements, their construction would have meant huge disruption to Anglo-Saxon towns. Norman cathedrals were established within Saxon towns and so the clearance of existing buildings was inevitable. When Bath Cathedral was rebuilt it is thought that about a quarter of the walled town was taken down for the precinct. Map evidence suggests that the main north–south street was truncated and redirected.[10] Clearly such bold actions must have had the full backing of the Crown in order to be implemented.

A good case study for these radical changes is Norwich. Here, the castle is known to have required the demolition of 98 houses and 2 churches, as is recorded in Domesday. The cathedral was built too late to be mentioned, but its position close to the market would have made it an obvious area for both houses and churches. Archaeology suggests that the late Saxon town had a gridded pattern of streets, with a major north–south road that aligned with the cathedral transepts. This road is thought to have intersected with an east–west Roman road (Holme St) around the position of the cathedral crossing.[11] In other words this new church was deliberately sited to block a major road junction. Recent excavations on the cathedral refectory site unearthed a road running diagonally underneath the Norman structures. This road was associated with buildings and yards and this was clearly a Late Saxon settlement. All evidence suggests that these buildings had been demolished, and then immediately built on in the form of the cathedral complex.[12] The archaeological evidence gives the impression of heavy handed treatment of the indigenous population. The clearance has all the hallmarks of compulsory purchase with probably little in the way of compensation. Yet the Normans may have just been expanding earlier ecclesiastical sites. In Norwich the large Saxon church of Holy Trinity is thought to have been just north of the current building so there was a precedent for building here. There may even have been an early monastery on the site as it shows some of the characteristics typical of monasteries.[13]

Despite the Norman zeal to replace Saxon buildings, they still saw the merits of stressing the past in order to give historical legitimacy to their sites. Completion of the Norman church was an opportunity for 'translating' the saints from the old Saxon churches to the new building. Norwich was especially keen to stress its roots with the old bishopric, as it was a new base for the see. It did this in a number of ways: the remains of the Anglo-Saxon bishop's throne from Elmham were transferred and set in a raised position east of the high altar (an outdated practice of the fifth century); an effigy of St Felix the missionary was erected over the north transept door; spiral piers marking the nave altar are thought to be a reference to the 'barley sugar stick' columns used around St Peter's shrine in Rome.[14] Even the very architecture of the Normans harked back to the past; the term Romanesque refers to its similarity to Roman architecture. This is seen in elements such as the round arches; and on an even larger scale the west front of Lincoln has been compared to a Roman triumphal arch. Of course many of these Norman buildings have since been substantially altered or completely rebuilt but the sites had been established. After the Normans the only completely new medieval cathedral to be built was Salisbury, founded in the early thirteenth century. Otherwise no new purpose-built cathedral, on a new site, was founded until Liverpool Anglican Cathedral in the twentieth century, apart from Truro, which retains some fabric from an earlier parish church.

The importance of cathedral shrines

Shrines were extremely important to people in the medieval period for a number of reasons. The first was connected with the doctrine of sin; pilgrimage to a shrine could be prescribed as a penance after confession. Even if a sin had not yet been committed, a trip to a shrine could earn the pilgrim an indulgence entitling him or her to a reduced stay in Purgatory. Other reasons to visit a shrine included begging the saint to intercede on your behalf on Judgement Day, or the belief that the bodies of the saints could transmit the healing powers of God. It was believed that a miraculous cure could be obtained by simply touching the shrine. This dependence was mutual since reliquary shrines were equally important to cathedrals. Their presence gave them increased prestige, sanctity and income. Those cathedrals without relics felt inadequate; during a visit to Fécamp, Bishop Hugh of Lincoln was driven to biting off a piece of Mary Magdalene's bone to take to his own cathedral. At the time of the Norman Conquest only 8 cathedrals had major shrines, and these were mostly tombs of early bishops such as St Cuthbert of Durham. However, by the time of the Reformation 14 of the 19 cathedrals had at least one major saint.[15] Of all these cathedral shrines, that of Thomas Becket at Canterbury was considered the most important in north-west Europe. How did this situation come about? The earliest Christian pilgrimages were probably to the tomb of St Peter, with which we began, and to the catacombs of Rome, but in Britain one of the earliest sites was the scene of St Alban's martyrdom. Bede wrote that these relics were visited by St Germanus of Auxerre in 429, which must be the first recorded pilgrimage in Britain.[16]

Christians are also credited with 'urbanizing' the dead. Although Roman temples were established in towns, by law all burials were kept outside the city walls. With Christianity the bodies of saints were brought into the city and most often placed near church altars, adding sanctity to the building. Relics fell into two classes: the actual bodily remains of the saint and objects closely associated with them. Prior to the Conquest the latter were more common due to the lack of home-grown saints, but later local saintly bones became more common.

Relics were in great demand and, as a consequence, some were, doubtless, of dubious origin; Calvin pointed out that there were enough relics of the True Cross to build a ship, and enough of the Crown of Thorns to hedge a field. In this context, a cathedral with the actual tomb of a saint had greater importance as a holy place.[17] The shrines housing these relics varied in form. Bede says that St Chad's tomb in Lichfield was a wooden house-shaped coffin with an aperture in the side where pilgrims could insert their hands and take holy dust. Shortcuts were occasionally taken. When a coffin was required for Etheldreda of Ely's first translation in 694, a masonry sarcophagus was requisitioned from a Roman cemetery in Cambridge.[18]

Owing to the destruction brought about by the Reformation, there are no surviving medieval reliquaries. All that remain are a few surviving shrine bases to give us an idea of how these great cathedral shrines would have looked. These bases were the means of elevating the reliquary. Archaeological study suggests that Norman shrines could have one of two forms; either a table type as that found at Canterbury, or a Foramina type. The latter was a stone chest pierced with large holes in the side. The tomb of St Osmund at Salisbury (complete but not in situ) and of St Swithin at Winchester (fragments) are of this type. It is thought they went out of vogue on account of the number of people who got stuck in the openings, in their enthusiasm to be close to the saint.[19] The approach to these shrines was also designed to add to a sense of occasion. Norwich and many other cathedrals had tall precinct walls which ensured that pilgrims were channelled in through one of the imposing gates which were decorated with statues. Visitors would then be directed towards the cathedral's west front and kept away from the other areas where the monks lived and worked. Archaeology suggests that there were internal walls to ensure people did not stray into the more private and sacred places of the cathedral priory.[20] Pilgrims would then probably have entered the nave, as this was the public area of the church. To gain access to the shrine itself they would have to pass several screens regulated by the shrine-keeper.

Shrines were situated in a number of places, the most common of which was in, or near, the High Altar. Most Norman shrines were behind the altar and – where there was an ambulatory – this allowed easy circulation for pilgrims paying their respects. Many cathedrals were rebuilt in the Gothic period, and the majority of those with shrines took the opportunity to build grand retrochoirs as, for example, in the Trinity Chapel at Canterbury for St Thomas Becket. Cathedral shrines were the 'holy of holies' and were therefore placed in the very heart of a church for sanctity and security. They would have been hidden from the laity by tall screens, such as the pulpitum at Ely, which added to their mystery. However, pilgrims still needed access and there are historical accounts of the disruption they caused. The chronicler of St William says his body was moved from the Norwich chapter house due to the number of pilgrims, and at St Denis near Paris the situation was far worse; Abbot Suger reported that the crowds coming to see the relics were so huge that people were 'squeezed as if in a winepress'. Occasionally, riots broke out and the monks would have to grab the relics and jump from the windows![21]

Shrines, saints and pilgrimage

Those most likely to be made saints and to be placed in cathedral shrines were bishops. This was often because they had dominated religion in life, and in death their remains were likely to be interred in the cathedral anyway. The living clergy were also more willing to spend money on the canonization of their own.[22] However, this process was still a gamble, and archaeology has uncovered an interesting example of a failed saint at Wells. William de Marchia was Bishop of Bath and Wells from 1293 to 1302. Wells was desperate for him to be canonized as it lacked a great saint, so a great shrine was built in anticipation, but, as it turns out, in vain. The attempt failed. In addition to his shrine, archaeologists have found his remains, crozier and chalice within a wall with a recess over. No doubt this recess was intended to display his relics.[23] Norwich had cults surrounding two bishops, but had another type of attraction too: a reputed boy martyr. William of Norwich was a 12-year-old apprentice skinner who was murdered in 1144. The killing was blamed on the Jews. William was promoted by the writings of one of the cathedral monks, Thomas of Monmouth, who wrote of his life and miracles. Lincoln had a similar boy martyr known as Little St Hugh; again the martyrdom was pinned on the significant Jewish population of the city.

People would travel long distances to visit cathedrals and their shrines. The journey was not just a penance, it was an opportunity to leave behind everyday things and to examine one's life from afar. The trip may have been timed to coincide with the festival of the saint when the whole city would participate in a fair. It is thought that most pilgrimages were simply short trips to a local shrine, so the closest cathedral would be an obvious port of call. Even this short journey would qualify as a pilgrimage; Margery Kempe of Lynn in Norfolk had been to Rome, Jerusalem and Compostela, yet still described a two-mile trip to a local shrine as a 'pilgrimage'. Overseas trips would have been most unusual; a pilgrimage to Canterbury might have been the most that ordinary people would have achieved in their life.[24]

Pilgrimage was a great leveller; all classes undertook these trips, as *The Canterbury Tales* shows – everyone from knight to ploughman went. Although the characters are fictional, Chaucer's tales, begun in 1388, form one of our best historical sources. Other useful evidence issues from the accounts and inventories of those in charge of shrine income and expenditure, such as the shrine-keeper and sacrist. Shrines were good money spinners. The Norwich sacrist's rolls are fairly complete from 1272 onwards and detail the offerings at all altars, shrines and images in the cathedral.[25] Pilgrims feature in the archaeological record too. Travellers would need accommodation or shelter en route to the cathedral shrines and so there would be a whole range of buildings scattered at intervals. These could range from church porches to bridge chapels, to hospitals, to inns. The grandest surviving pilgrim inns are the New Inn at Gloucester and the George & Pilgrim at Glastonbury.[26]

Once pilgrims arrived, Benedictine cathedrals such as Norwich would have been obliged to offer hospitality to all, since the Rule of St Benedict requires that everyone should be 'received as if they are Christ'. A boss over the eastern entrance to the hostry at Norwich depicts an open door to symbolize this. There was, however, a sliding scale of welcome; high-ranking guests were entertained by the prior in his lodgings, clerics would stay in the hostry and eat in the refectory, whereas ordinary pilgrims would probably be billeted close to the main gates. Archaeological analysis shows that in the hostry there was probably a large open communal hall with two-storeyed private chambers at either end, one of which connected with a chapel. All the necessary en-suite requirements of a clergyman were provided.[27] Successful shrines would need increased accommodation for visiting pilgrims and detached guest halls were built in the later Middle Ages.[28]

One of the most interesting pilgrim souvenirs discovered at a shrine is a prayer card on vellum showing the Bromholm Cross; this souvenir, from Bromholm Priory, Norfolk, could be one of the earliest postcards discovered. The more usual souvenirs were pilgrim badges, small lead or pewter images of the relevant saint. Despite their fragile nature, around 1,300 of these have been found in England alone. This is evidence of numerous pilgrimages.[29] Excavations at Worcester Cathedral have revealed something more interesting still. A fifteenth-century grave was discovered containing a male skeleton. This person has been identified as a pilgrim as he showed signs of having been an experienced walker and was buried with sturdy boots and a staff.[30] This pilgrim either died during his visit to Worcester, or was a local known for such trips. Cathedral shrines were of great significance in the medieval period. To the pilgrim the shrine was a place where miracles could occur, indulgences might be granted, and penances redeemed. Making the journey there would cleanse the soul. For the cathedral the shrine increased prestige, holiness and income.

Informing the future: the conservation of cathedrals

Since 1990 cathedrals have been expected to employ archaeologists and archivists to advise them as required by the Care of Cathedrals Measure. This was a move to ensure that cathedrals benefit from expert advice from leading authorities about the historical nature of their buildings. Even the standing elements of a cathedral must be considered as archaeology; the discipline is no longer restricted to structures below ground. It is now recognized that it is just as important to record repairs and alterations to the *standing* historic fabric, as to that which is revealed by excavation.[31] Cathedral archaeology is therefore now defined as the complete historical study of the fabric and material remains – above and below ground – and includes its site, contents and historical setting. Having seen the respect people gave cathedrals in the past it is important to remember that these buildings reflect the whole of society and not just those who lived and worked within the precinct. Cathedrals bear the imprints of political and religious influences, the most obvious examples being Norman domination and the power struggle of the Reformation.

Archivists work to conserve original documents relating to the building and bring them to the attention of scholars. Historians then consult this documentary evidence and publish everything from the translated monastic accounts to collections of essays celebrating a particular anniversary since the foundation. The dissemination of scholarly work makes the cathedral's history more accessible to all, whether they be students, researchers or, simply, interested visitors. Likewise, the detailed work of the archaeologist interprets the past through excavation or through studying the standing building while it is being repaired. Excavation at Norwich has shown the disruption caused by the construction of the Norman building; analysis of the hostry remains has informed us about the manner in which pilgrims were accommodated. These disciplines aid the cathedral in its role as educator. They are educationally all inclusive, spanning those clutching their copies of Pevsner's *The Buildings of England* all the way across to schoolchildren.

These historical disciplines also contribute much to the actual repair and conservation of the building. Without archives it is impossible to know precisely what work took place in the past and how decisions were made then. Archives can range from the medieval rolls to modern chapter minutes. The most relevant for the fabric are those deposited by the architect, which can take the form of drawings, correspondence and photographs. This is an invaluable record of the changes to the building, and even modern records can provide a unique insight into evidence that has been lost. The Norwich archive contains a single tantalizing photograph documenting the medieval scissor-framed roof of the cathedral which was removed without trace in the 1950s and 1960s. Without an archive this information would be lost to us. The archive is also important for assessing which materials were used and whether these are still appropriate. Some processes used in the past are now seen as detrimental and need to be reversed. So, the Norwich cloister was painted with sealant in the early twentieth century to protect the stonework. This treatment prevents the stone from breathing and traps moisture inside, so must be removed. Some of the bosses too have been painted with modern paint which has caused a similar problem.

Survey work is a further contribution of cathedral archaeologists. Accurate, detailed plans are needed by the cathedral architect in order to specify areas of repairs and conservation. Archaeologists can provide this specialism since it is in their interests to record the building, both to create a record before work begins and also to plot any interesting historical discoveries. Both requirements, of the architect and archaeologist, are complementary, demanding high accuracy. The recording of the Norwich hostry is an example of this collaboration. Accurate information about the historic elevations was required in advance of the design of a new visitors' centre and the conservation of the walls. Survey and photographic methods were used to produce 'photo-realistic' drawings of the 55-metre-long wall which were then turned into traditional line drawings. This satisfied all of the architect's needs, and was also used to plot the position of former and existing features, such as the Romanesque windows, as they were revealed during conservation.

This work is paralleled in the Norwich Measured Survey. This pilot project produced floor plans of the cathedral at seven levels, from basement to roof. It was carried out using modern survey equipment and achieved an accuracy to within a few millimetres over the 141-metre building. It was the first modern survey of an English cathedral. The archaeological incentive for this project was to study the layout of the building, accurately mapped for the first time. It is now possible to 'look through walls' and see how features relate to one another. As this is a digital survey, it is also possible to obtain dimensions from the plans and therefore to study the proportions used in its design. The 'real' stimulus for this project was to produce an accurate record of the existing historic building so that new visitor facilities could be built within the footprint of the ruined cloister buildings. The plans achieved that aim and have since been used to provide the necessary detail in preparing for floor replacement, conservation and the repair of cloister roofs. The success is such that English Heritage is encouraging measured surveys in all cathedrals. Archaeology and archives therefore make a valuable contribution to the conservation of the cathedral, and, in addition to this, these disciplines can help cathedrals reinforce their significance and adjust to a new role in the future.

As the centre of the diocese, and with more resources and visitors than other churches in the region, the cathedral can set an example and spearhead new initiatives. These skills, and the insights of specialists, will then filter across to other churches and historic buildings.

There remains a very strong focus upon, and care for, our nation's cathedrals, even though we live in a very different age and culture. In medieval times there was a real sense of religious dependence and devotion, driven by the nature of the society in which people then lived. Nevertheless, the number of people visiting cathedrals in the twenty-first century is probably greater than at any time in past ages. Cathedrals now actively serve the local community, doing work almost as a 'chaplaincy' to the city, country and region in which they are placed, and providing a key focus at times of national and local celebration or mourning. Our reflection on the increasing archaeological understanding of cathedrals and their origin has become a key component in our interpretation and care of these great buildings. Archaeology has helped us to understand better the way in which cathedrals were originally established, but also the way in which they developed over the centuries. As well as being the seat of the bishop, they became the site of shrines of local and internationally acclaimed saints, and so became the focus of a broader devotion still. Alongside this, however, they also were used at various points in history as part of the means of government by the presiding overlords. The changes that happened following the Norman conquest are a classical example of this, but cathedrals continued to play a significant part thereafter. This was made clear in the way that Henry VIII refounded cathedrals during the first part of the sixteenth-century Reformation. The continuing importance of cathedrals, following the English Reformation, has given them a unique place in English society. Archaeology and historical study, alongside the use of archives, has helped us to understand better the way in which cathedrals have developed. This in itself also gives pointers to the future as to how we can develop them further, in an undeniably different age where the focus on the remains of saints and their shrines no longer dominates people's consciousness.

Ironically, this brings us back to the place where we began, to the burial of Pope John Paul II. It was fascinating to see such remarkable coverage from this nation's media and, indeed, across the world. It indicates that, in a rather different manner, cathedrals still play a very significant part in society in focusing people's emotion and understanding of human existence. Perhaps these recent events, and others like them, may help us, with the assistance of archaeological study, to see even more clearly how cathedrals can contribute in the future.[32]

Notes

1 T. Tatton-Brown, *The English Cathedral* (London, New Holland, 2002), p. 50.

2 J. Schofield, 'The Archaeology of St Paul's Cathedral up to 1666', *Church Archaeology*, Volumes 5 and 6 (2004), pp. 5–12 (6).

3 Cf. D. Webb, *Pilgrimage in Medieval England* (London, Hambledon and London, 2000), p. 3.

4 W. Rodwell, 'Above and Below Ground: Archaeology at Wells Cathedral', in T. Tatton-Brown and J. Munby (eds), *The Archaeology of Cathedrals* (Oxford, Oxford University Committee for Archaeology, 1996), pp. 115–34; Rodwell, *Wells Cathedral: Excavations and Structural Studies, 1978–93* (London, English Heritage, 2001), as reviewed by John Blair in *Church Archaeology*, Volumes 5 and 6 (2004), pp. 134–5.

5 Tatton-Brown, *The English Cathedral*, pp. 10–11.

6 J. Maddison, *Ely Cathedral: Design and Meaning* (Ely, Ely Cathedral Publications, 2000), p. 6.

7 Tatton-Brown, *The English Cathedral*, p. 11.

8 Tatton-Brown, *The English Cathedral*, pp. 65–72.

9 Tatton-Brown, *The English Cathedral*, p. 56; Maddison, *Ely Cathedral*, p. 12.

10 P. Davenport, 'The Cathedral Priory Church at Bath', in Tatton-Brown and Munby (eds), *The Archaeology of Cathedrals*, pp. 19–39 (19).

11 B. Ayers, *Norwich: 'A Fine City'* (Stroud, Tempus, 2003), p. 54.

12 H. Wallis, 'Excavations on the site of Norwich Cathedral Refectory 2001–2003', *East Anglian Archaeology* (forthcoming).

13 R. Gilchrist, *Norwich Cathedral Close: The Evolution of the English Cathedral Landscape* (Woodbridge, Boydell & Brewer, 2005).

14 E. Fernie, *An Architectural History of Norwich Cathedral* (Oxford, Oxford University Press, 1993).

15 B. Nilson, *Cathedral Shrines of Medieval England* (Woodbridge, Boydell & Brewer, 1998).

16 Webb, *Pilgrimage in Medieval England*, p. 1.

17 Nilson, *Cathedral Shrines of Medieval England*, p. 3.

18 Maddison, *Ely Cathedral*, p 5.

19 J. Crook, 'Recent Archaeology in Winchester Cathedral', in Tatton-Brown and Munby (eds), *The Archaeology of Cathedrals*, pp. 135–51 (146).

20 Gilchrist – personal comment.

21 P. Binski, *Medieval Death* (London, The British Museum Press, 1996), p. 18.

22 Nilson, *Cathedral Shrines of Medieval England*, p. 10.

23 Rodwell, 'Above and Below Ground', p. 127.

24 Webb, *Pilgrimage in Medieval England*, p. xiii.

25 J. R. Shinners, 'The Veneration of Saints at Norwich Cathedral in the Fourteenth Century', *Norfolk Archaeology* (1988), pp. 133–44 (134).

26 Webb, *Pilgrimage in Medieval England*, pp. 221–5.

27 Gilchrist, *Norwich Cathedral Close*.

28 J. Crook, 'The Pilgrim's Hall, Worcester: Hammerbeams, Base Crucks and Aisle-derivative Roof Structures', *Archaeologia*, 109 (1991), pp. 129–59.

29 Nilson, *Cathedral Shrines of Medieval England*, p. 112.

30 Webb, *Pilgrimage in Medieval England*, p. 212.

31 Tatton-Brown and Munby (eds), *The Archaeology of Cathedrals*.

32 My thanks to Professor Roberta Gilchrist for her valuable comments on this chapter.

9

Conservation and renewal

JANE KENNEDY

In 1988 Alan Bennett recorded a visit to Ely:

> Then to Ely where I have not been since I cycled there thirty five years
> ago . . . In 1953 the cathedral was damp and empty, looming like a
> liner out of the fog. Now there is a desk inside the door and it costs
> £1.60 to go in, which I don't mind much – less, anyway, than the infor-
> mation display that spills, as it does in all such places, halfway down
> the north aisle, like 'Who's Who in the Diocese of Ely', a montage of
> photos from Bishop to Verger, all flashing fluorescent smiles. 'That's
> nice' says a visitor and I suppose it's just me that minds . . .[1]

How can we develop our cathedrals for worship and mission and at
the same time retain the sense of sacred space which attracts so many
of us to them? In the last 20 years from the time of writing all cathedrals have worked hard to reach their wider communities, to explain
and teach the faith to worshippers and visitors and to create a sense of
welcome for all. This has inevitably meant more notices, display
boards, welcomers, shops, cafés and exhibitions: all to some extent
intruding into the buildings. In their turn they produce even more
visitors, more guided tours, school parties and disturbance of the
place for concerts, rehearsals and plays. Then, sooner or later comes
the demand for a new building to house some of these activities and
the paraphernalia they require.

Successful 'marketing' of our cathedrals can bring so many visitors
that the sense of calm can be lost. Westminster Abbey and Canterbury
Cathedral have both introduced entrance charges in order to limit the
numbers of visitors and 'recover the calm'. Smaller cathedrals and

those off the tourists' beaten track often find they must charge if they are to keep open. Cathedrals which have to make an entrance charge feel obliged to offer their visitors more: more guided tours, shops and other facilities in competition with secular 'visitor attractions'. Cathedrals become busier and more cluttered by the 'hardware' added in order to help visitors. Turnstiles and cash registers, even in a cathedral shop, seem out of place and remind us of Christ's angry reaction to the traders in the Temple.

Why does this matter? Notices, even of welcome, can be obtrusive if poorly designed. Extensive displays illustrating the life and work of the Church, however beautifully created, take up valuable space, impinge on the historic architecture and therefore often detract from what we want our visitors to experience. Guided tours, lively school parties and concert rehearsals can bring life to a quiet place, but they can equally destroy the atmosphere for the solitary pilgrim. Even simple physical adaptations to make buildings accessible to those in wheelchairs and prams can be at odds with ancient doors and flights of stairs. Must we go along with all these developments; why do cathedrals need to develop in the manner of museums and stately homes?

Cathedrals need to attract visitors and, whether or not an entrance charge is made, one of the chief reasons for welcoming them is to obtain income from them. Effective welcome requires good reception for visitors, worshippers and pilgrims. With greater mobility and relative affluence there are potentially more visitors to cathedrals than ever before. Cathedrals are working in an increasingly competitive 'market' and compete with many other 'heritage' attractions. But many visitors have relatively little knowledge of the Christian faith or understanding of European architectural history. They must first be made to feel welcome and then given the opportunity to learn about the buildings. To provide that opportunity requires advertising, directional signs, welcome boards, maps, lists of opening times and information to be given about the architecture and history of the building and its current life. It can be done very simply if the circulation route is right, and a good welcomer can be the best source of information, although it remains true that in most places there are much more extensive signs, display boards and exhibitions than that seen by Alan Bennett in Ely in 1988.

Providing information for visitors gives one type of access to the building. Some visitors find it difficult to enter the buildings because they are in wheelchairs or push a pram. Others need interpretation because they are blind or deaf or have learning difficulties. Chapters (the administrative bodies of cathedrals) wish to make people feel welcome and included, but to do so can mean physical alterations such as ramps or new doorways and the addition of more interpretative materials such as the excellent model cathedrals for the blind.

But we do not welcome only tourists: chapters wish to ensure that cathedrals are at the heart of their dioceses and will be able to reach out to the local community, the city and the county. There are often significant social issues and local needs to be met especially in the larger urban centres. So, once again, there may be a need for new building or adapted space for community use and almost certainly for separate facilities for school visits.

An effective education programme and expanding arts use for theatre, concerts and exhibitions will fill the cathedral with more occasions for interrupting the peace. Arts use and changing liturgies can make demands on the furnishing and ordering of the buildings as well as requiring ancillary support facilities including storage areas for staging and chairs. How have cathedrals coped with the demands of development? Can growth be accommodated without affecting the sense of the sacred? Can we effectively defend the sense of spaciousness in our cathedrals? If we can contain the essential visitor facilities can we also ensure that the space is not filled with piles of chairs and other clutter? Many cathedrals are meticulously cared for and the sense of order is palpable, but others can be a complete mess. Good liturgy needs dignified space; the spiritual sense in a place will be destroyed if the aisles are always full of the paraphernalia of vergers and cleaners.

In this chapter I will look at recent developments in cathedrals in the light of the legislative controls, new thoughts on conservation planning and new sources of funding. I will assess their success in meeting the demands of clergy wishing both to reach out to visitors and work creatively in the buildings without detracting from the buildings themselves and the sense of order and calm which they should maintain.

Andrew Anderson in *Flagships of the Spirit* wrote eloquently on the history of our cathedral buildings, and their continuing care and repair.[2] There is little more to be said about the maintenance of these buildings, but since he wrote there have been significant changes in the way that cathedrals are governed, and the controls which apply to their conservation and adaptation have developed in use. There have also been changes to the ways that such work is funded, and recent work in cathedrals should be assessed in the light of such changes.

Cathedrals, like parish churches, are exempt from secular 'listed building' legislation. For centuries works to churches have been subject to the Anglican Church's own form of planning procedures by which a parish must apply for a 'Faculty' to carry out repairs or alterations and to sell or acquire any significant furnishings. Cathedrals were brought into a similar control system in 1990 when the Care of Cathedrals Measure established both local Fabric Advisory Committees and a national Cathedrals Fabric Commission. Chapters must apply to these two bodies for permission to repair or alter cathedrals and for any works which affect the archaeology of the cathedral or the precinct. The Measure also requires chapters to appoint a cathedral architect to carry out quinquennial inspections of the cathedral and the chapter must also ensure that precinct properties are inspected and reported upon every five years. A new measure enacted in 2005 tightens controls on applications for repair and maintenance. Both Faculty Jurisdiction and the Cathedrals Measure are altogether more stringent than the secular Listed Building Legislation and they have together ensured high standards of scholarship, repair and creative adaptations to church buildings.

There is nothing in the United Kingdom comparable to the funding for administration and maintenance of cathedrals provided by the State in France or by Church taxes in, for example, Germany and Denmark. Members of the public often believe that in some way the State supports our churches; the reality is that the small amounts of money which have been available for maintaining and repairing our built heritage have been significantly reduced in recent years. While this is also a problem shared with parish churches and with the cathedrals, churches and chapels of other denominations, it is surely most significant for the historic Anglican cathedrals. However, hand in hand with the Cathedrals Measure in 1991 came English Heritage's cathedrals grants scheme which has given over £40 million towards repair of both Anglican and Roman Catholic cathedrals in England. English Heritage has insisted on applicants producing five-year plans for repairs, and this regime has resulted in much clearer planning for repair, maintenance and development. The chapter at Lincoln, for example, one of our largest and most important medieval buildings, for many years struggled to cope with the repair needs. Small rusting scaffolds apparently haphazardly dotted about the structure indicated that not enough money was available to carry out comprehensive repairs and nor was there any planned campaign to coordinate what could be afforded. In many cathedrals grants have been the catalyst for fundraising and have thus ensured that urgent and necessary repairs were planned logically and undertaken with care. This can be demonstrated by comparing the results of surveys which English Heritage commissioned from Harry Fairhurst in 1991 and 2001. By 2001 85 per cent of the urgent work identified ten years previously had been done. The level of grant aid offered by English Heritage has now dropped dramatically and this will have significant consequences for Lincoln and other major buildings still needing support to complete necessary repairs. There is, however, a real level of understanding between English Heritage officials, cathedral administrations and their architects, which supports a constructive and creative approach to maintenance and repairs. And in Lincoln there has now been a sustained period of well-planned and effective repairs.

The National Lottery, now over ten years old, has also been able to grant funds through the Arts Council, the Heritage Lottery Fund and the Millennium Commission. Money from these sources is usually directed towards development work rather than repair. These bodies demand that substantial preparation be undertaken when applying for grants, often including the commissioning of a 'Conservation Management Plan' before proposals for change are discussed. This type of plan requires first an understanding of the place, the buildings and their significance and then the creation of policies for the retention and enhancement of significance. It is a rigorous process which should involve the community and should mean that development can follow in an orderly fashion without destroying the special qualities of the place that is to be developed. There are as yet few cathedral conservation plans, but the understanding which they promote is clearly evident in those recent schemes which are discussed below.

What has been the effect of these changes in legislation and funding? Cathedrals have had to become more accountable to the secular heritage bodies. This accountability is paralleled by the changes to their own statutes and governance: the introduction of the laity onto chapters and the institution of Cathedral Councils to give supervision and advice. However, at the same time there have been greater opportunities to obtain significant funding. Chapters have been more likely to make substantial repairs and additions to their buildings than at any time during the last century and the rate of change and investment has been similar to the great nineteenth-century church and cathedral 'restorations'.

These changes are also better managed. Chapters cannot rush into alterations. It takes time to commission the conservation plan and detailed design and archaeological appraisals needed to support an application under the Care of Cathedrals Measure and to apply for funding. Fabric Advisory Committees do not meet very often and they and the Cathedrals Fabric Commission for England (the parent body) often ask for changes and resubmissions. English Heritage and/ or the amenity societies make comments which have to be addressed. Any alterations that go ahead need to be well thought out or they will stumble at these hurdles.

We should therefore look at recent work in cathedrals in the light of these changes in legislation and funding. Has the work been carefully planned? Was it necessary? How has it helped the cathedrals' mission to visitors and outreach to the community? Does it enhance and complement the older buildings? Finally, has it retained or reclaimed the sacred space and the calm, or even neglect, so much enjoyed by Alan Bennett?

Many of our cathedrals have undertaken building work to meet the developing needs of their communities. These range from the completion of St Edmundsbury with a soaring Gothic tower to make the cathedral a landmark in the Suffolk landscape, and the masterly completion of the exterior setting of Liverpool's Roman Catholic cathedral, to Southwark's fine rebuilding of a range of ancillary buildings in an exciting urban setting.

In assessing the 'success' of any development it is useful to ask questions about the scheme's gestation, usefulness and quality. In the following detailed studies of seven very different places and the work which has been done or is planned to be done there, these questions are asked:

- Is the scheme a new building, an adaptation of existing space or a combination of the two?
- Is it built on the footprint of the previous (monastic?) building? (While there are sometimes justifications for developing on a new site, a building most often sits comfortably and logically if it is 'knitted' into the medieval plan.)
- What is its main purpose?
- How long was it in gestation and planning and what was the quality of that planning? Hastily thought-up schemes are rarely right for the place; slower development allows the ideas to be refined and for a real archaeological and theological understanding to guide the development.
- Is the scheme of high quality in construction and detailing?
- Does the project solve just one or a range of problems and in particular has it in some way accommodated new life while reclaiming the calm?

Norwich Cathedral refectory

At Norwich there has been built a fine new restaurant within the site of the medieval refectory. This is the first phase of a scheme to provide visitor facilities within the monastic building. In so doing it has given life to one of the country's finest surviving cloisters. The result is that visitors are dispersed and the cloister walks reinstated as places that lead to other buildings. The design was chosen in an architectural competition and the resulting building, by Michael Hopkins, is one of the best modern insertions into a historic building in the UK. Its construction has enabled the opening of an old entry in the southeast corner of the cloister and thus created a new route for visitors into the buildings and it has also extended and rejuvenated the cathedral library.

A second phase, the hostry, will be developed within the footprint of medieval buildings abutting the cloister and will provide shop, meeting room and song school. Educational facilities will be housed in the adjoining medieval west range of the cloister. It is accepted that visitors approach the cathedral from a number of different directions; the cloister will help to orientate them while commerce and busyness will be accommodated outside the church itself. The whole scheme is an excellent example of the subtle dispersal of visitors and activity, maintaining the atmosphere within the cathedral church yet providing extensive facilities for many uses within a straightforward and logical development.

The work has progressed hand in hand with a campaign of repair to the medieval fabric under the direction of the cathedral architect, and he in turn has worked with the Chapter, English Heritage and the Cathedrals Fabric Commission with a shared vision for the care, development and presentation of the cathedral.

All the work is of the highest architectural quality and the developments use the monastic building logically and thoughtfully. Much is provided for the comfort and interest of visitors but the atmosphere of the church itself remains intact.

Sheffield

Sheffield is a 'parish church' cathedral: a substantial medieval building which became a cathedral in 1913. In the twentieth century there were four phases of enlargement and extension. The building is now enhanced by the creation of a landscaped forecourt in the city centre, and a great deal of work is done with the homeless and the disadvantaged. For some 15 years and with successive deans and chapters, plans have been developed by the cathedral architect for a significant extension to bring some liturgical order to the church on a west–east axis and to develop social and community uses on a north–south axis.

Developments are outside the medieval footprint and follow no historic precedent. The scheme has evolved slowly and work was due to begin in 2005. It will knit together the disparate spaces of the interior and integrate the social outreach work with the gatherings of the worshipping community. Access will be improved and clarity will be given to the place of the church itself. The solutions here will surely comprise a most exciting contemporary development.

Salisbury

The sudden availability of large sums of money from the National Lottery persuaded several cathedrals to consider 'grand projects' in the 1990s. Bradford secured millennium funding and developed a major new centre which failed through lack of planning either for its use or for raising revenue funding. The lottery distributors are now more stringent in their demand for business plans. At Salisbury there was an idea to build a Magna Carta centre and an architectural competition was held. Ideas and funding developed slowly and in the meantime the essential visitor facilities (shop, restaurant and lavatories) were becoming inadequate and a temporary solution was sought.

Shop, restaurant and other facilities have been built into the space known as the 'Plumbery', a former works yard between the nave and cloister. It is a simple and elegant lean-to building with a glazed roof. It is designed to be reversible in that all can be removed with little effect on the surviving medieval walls to north and south. But with an understanding that what is intended as temporary often remains for many years it was built to the highest quality. It was never intended that this building would solve many problems but it was a simple and entirely logical way to proceed while the long-term development evolved. It was designed by the cathedral architects and its success owes much to their deep understanding of the buildings which surround it. The 'Plumbery' restaurant may well outlive its ten-year planned life and the eventual development might as a result be phased, but this is an excellent start.

Chester

Chester retains an extensive range of monastic buildings which have been adapted for visitor uses in recent years. Here a new Song School has been built over the surviving parlour and in the space once occupied by the monks' dormitory. It is approached appropriately for processional use via the medieval day stairs although there is a separate external entrance and lift access.

The building was planned over many years and by two successive cathedral architects and negotiated over time with the Cathedrals Fabric Commission. The second of these architects was in post for two years before he started work and the sensitivity and success of the building arise from his careful study and understanding of the place. It is of high quality, being built in red sandstone with good oak interior joinery and the two main spaces, large and small rehearsal rooms, are both delightful, as is the attic music library and office with a trefoil window looking out across the cloister. The building can be used for receptions, recitals and rehearsals when not occupied by a choir, and the parlour beneath will have a new lease of life as a meeting and conference facility.

It cannot be said that this building will affect the experience of the visitor or pilgrim to Chester except that it does allow two different groups to rehearse without being on the cathedral floor. It provides a first-rate facility for musicians and will certainly expand that aspect of the cathedral's life. It is also a flexible space which can be used for cathedral gatherings and commercial conferences without impinging on the cathedral floor or the cloister and is a natural reinstatement of medieval spaces.

It is a fine building, constructed within the monastic precinct, designed with a great understanding of the place. It accommodates a great deal of activity which adds to the mission and life of the church but without impinging on the experience of the church itself.

St Paul's

St Paul's Cathedral, like Canterbury and Westminster, has huge numbers of visitors. The cathedral floor is always busy but for many years was cluttered and poorly divided to provide a shop and entrance desks which filled the west end and distracted visitor and worshipper alike. Facilities were otherwise minimal and the vast crypt was occupied by a miscellany of stores and a staff canteen.

The solution which evolved over a number of years was to clear out the crypt and adapt it to provide dignified visitor access to a new restaurant and shop, lavatories, conference and education facilities and an appropriate approach to the monuments and the OBE Chapel at the east end of the building. There is gathering and meeting space and all, including fittings, are to a high quality, designed by the surveyor.

Few cathedrals have such convenient spaces to develop, so this is not a universally practical example (except for Blackburn whose similarly extensive crypt may be developed for visitor and community work once an exciting scheme to develop the precinct is underway). However, the quality of the thinking behind the scheme, the use of space and the delight in its details are exceptional. There is no sense that visitors are being sent down to the basement to use basic facilities; they are now guided there to experience a series of well-presented 'rooms' and spaces beautifully fitted and adapted for their new purposes.

With commerce and secular uses relegated to the crypt, the cathedral floor has reclaimed its dignity and the experience of the visitor and worshipper is enhanced. A coordinated programme of work here, including the creation of a raised platform under the nave, the painstaking cleaning of the inside of the building and a new lighting scheme, is giving coherence and spiritual and liturgical meaning to the interior.

Wells

Wells Cathedral is working on a scheme which is described as the opposite of a visitor centre: 'a visitor disperse'. Initially commissioned to design one building to solve all problems, the architect has evolved a scheme which uses the many ancillary spaces of the cathedral to provide accommodation for shop, refectory, song school, stone store, and a space in which groups can arrive and orientate themselves. In so doing the cloister walks, currently occupied, or rather blocked, by refectory, shop and furniture stores, will be reopened. A logical circulation pattern, beginning at the west doors, will be re-established.

A new building will be constructed for shop and refectory within an existing walled garden just to the south-west of the cathedral. Groups will enter here but the overall physical impact will not seem significant because it will happen behind the garden walls. This scheme, which is due to be constructed in the next few years, will be significant not only for the quality of the new architecture but for its rethinking and reworking of how visitors and the resident community use the buildings.

The scheme has arisen from quite a different brief from that at Sheffield; both will, however, not only provide significant new facilities for their communities and visitors but also reinstate logical circulation routes and enhance the liturgical space. They are almost certainly the two most interesting and exciting developments now taking place in English cathedrals.

Ely

If Alan Bennett remembers damp at Ely in the 1950s, he was probably thinking of the Lady Chapel, a large, almost detached rectangular building with vast windows and the most delicately and ornately carved interior. It was unheated for many years and was not infrequently, in the winter months, colder inside than out. It has an exceptional acoustic and is much loved for singing though not for speech. It was entered through a doorway cut through the medieval masonry at its west end; one 'slid' into the building through a hole in the corner since the central medieval entrance was blocked after the Reformation. Recently the chapel's use has been transformed by the reconstruction of the medieval passageway which leads from the cathedral choir to the chapel (the traditional pilgrim route), and by taking up a twentieth-century patchwork floor in the chapel itself, and laying a new patterned pavement with underfloor heating.

The medieval entrance in the centre of the south wall has thus been reinstated, with a ramped access passage constructed using Gothic geometry. The passageway is built upon the foundations of its medieval predecessor. It is a stone building in a simple modern Gothic style with a green oak roof, fine carved roof bosses and interesting glazing. The Lady Chapel floor is laid in contrasting Purbeck 'marbles' using medieval patterns. All has been built well yet the work in over-all terms is modest. The chapel has a simple sound reinforcement system which helps for speech. The new heating system means that it can now be used throughout the year for choral evensong and compline, concerts, meetings and other events. Alongside the new passage entrance is a kitchen, and the chapel is occasionally used for dinners.

These developments have 'opened up' the Lady Chapel for winter use and enabled the dispersal of visitors. The development should be seen alongside the purchase and adaptation for educational use of the former public library opposite the west front of the cathedral; this provides a base and teaching rooms for visiting schoolchildren and adult parties.

Alan Bennett will, however, still regret that Ely's shop takes up four bays of the north aisle and that despite many attempts to simplify the signage and information boards these seem to be ever on the increase!

Within the last 20 years (at the time of writing) about half of the Anglican cathedrals in England have undertaken substantial new works, in most cases to provide facilities for visitors (although there are often other benefits). In a few, such as Chester's Song School or the completion of Portsmouth, the work has been principally for the purpose of worship. Portsmouth pioneered change for liturgical purposes. New lighting schemes are now being installed in a number of places, with both subtlety and great flexibility of control; they allow space and architecture to be presented in a variety of ways, giving changes of mood and focus which can enhance both liturgical and secular uses. That these developments have been possible says a great deal for the workings of the Cathedrals Measure and the understanding and cooperation of English Heritage and the amenity societies. It clearly demonstrates that cathedrals can make bold and creative decisions and that the public will support them financially.

Looked at together, the schemes discussed above strike an appropriate balance between providing visitor facilities and attempting to reclaim or maintain the sense of the sacred. This is most dramatically achieved at St Paul's. In other places, such as Norwich, increasing numbers of groups are being absorbed without damaging the peace of the solitary pilgrim.

The best work is not necessarily grand. Simple schemes such as those at Chester, Ely and Wells can be just as effective as a major intervention. The long-term relationship which cathedral architects normally enjoy with clients has ensured that 'conservation planning' has happened naturally. This is exemplified first by a scholarly understanding of place and buildings, then a holistic analysis of the issues and the development of integrated policies for development. Great projects which are designed to glorify one particular dean are now unlikely to find approval.

Cathedrals do have their own special purpose and should not be in competition for visitors with museums or country houses. The successful schemes described here are models not only for other cathedrals and churches but also for a broad range of tourist attractions: both historic buildings and landscapes. They illustrate that cathedrals' commitment to quality and ability to take the long view will result in sensitive additions which benefit both visitors and cathedral communities. What is more, changes can be made without destroying what is sacred.

The schemes I have described are not 'grand projects' but logical and careful developments and infillings of complex, mainly medieval, plans. They provide facilities to enhance and support the mission and worship of the cathedrals. They may have radically changed the ways in which the buildings are used, but they have done so without needing to repeat the great rebuildings or 'restorations' of the nineteenth and mid-twentieth centuries.

Notes

1 Alan Bennett, *Writing Home* (London, Faber and Faber, 1994), pp. 161–2.
2 S. Platten and C. Lewis (eds), *Flagships of the Spirit* (London, Darton, Longman and Todd, 1998), Chapter 6, 'Building and Cherishing: Cathedrals as Buildings', pp. 90–104.

10

*Les grands projets**

JAMES ATWELL

———••◆••———

The autumn mist is descending and darkness is settling over the
Suffolk town of Bury St Edmunds. Among the abbey ruins through
the swirling veil appear stark white fingers stabbing upwards. They
look as if trying to grasp a glory that has vanished, their hands reaching from the ground before Hades drowns and stills any final gesture
of defiance. When the autumn sun drives away the mist the following
morning the stabbing fingers are seen to be the flint and rubble
remains of once-proud columns. One of the medieval glories of
England, a religious house whose abbot stood shoulder to shoulder
with the Abbot of Cluny, has vanished. Farm carts have long since
carried off the hewn stones to supply the little projects of busyness,
their carters without a lingering thought of the great vision they dis-
mantled. Abbots like Baldwin appointed in 1065, a Frenchman before
his time, Anselm nephew of the great Archbishop, the red-haired and
headstrong Samson all lusted after the great project. They wanted
their abbey to be a monument grander, larger and more impressive
for the glory of God, yes, but also as a sign of power to impress a wary
world.

Have we not learned the lessons of time? Adjacent to these ruins a
modest church-in-waiting on the once great abbey is raising its head
as a cathedral. Another great endeavour is underway as a lantern
tower is built above the crossing in the best traditions of medieval
masonry in stone and mortar to last a thousand years. Should we

---

* '*Les grands projets*' was a phrase coined by François Mitterand, President of France,
  to describe the great building projects in Paris including the Louvre pyramid, the
  Pompidou Centre and La Défense.

perhaps have understood that 'small is beautiful',[1] that grand gestures are empty and nowadays no-one is impressed? There have been voices raised to express this view. The column inches of the local press have noted how a ward for the local hospital might have been a more appropriate millennial gesture. Yet, 'without a vision the people perish' (Proverbs 29.18). If hospitals are to be built and people cared for then a vision which insists these things are worth doing has to be sustained. It is necessary for there to be visible statements in our environment that point us upwards to some higher goal than the satisfied customer.

There is a major difference between the Romanesque builders of Bury St Edmunds and their contemporary successors. The Church builds today from weakness and not from strength. The abbot in times past was a baron whose word was literally life or death for the inhabitants of his bailiwick. The historian Antonia Gransden remarks of the building of the great Romanesque churches of the Anglo-Norman era: 'Each such church was a statement of ecclesiastical power, both that of the church concerned and that of the new regime of which it was an integral part.'[2] The cathedral chapter of the present has no great wealth or contemporary secular authority. The building of a tower is no longer cloaked with a hidden message that demands submission. It simply edges a statement alongside the brewery chimneys, the silos of British Sugar and the clock tower of the multistorey car park. Because of the contemporary weakness of the Church the statement in stone 'lift up your hearts' is ironically clearer and stronger. St Paul captured the Christian insight 'when I am weak, then I am strong' (2 Corinthians 12.10). Maybe it is a lesson that today's Church should take to heart. Being weak and vulnerable gives opportunities. People are more likely to listen to a voice which shares their weakness than to one that is strident and above the ordinary perplexities of life. We may dare *les grands projets* provided we realize that we build from weakness and to serve rather than to impress.

Cathedrals may not be a new way of expressing Christian mission, but they are a different and distinctive presence within the national Church. The English Reformation lost the monastic orders, which were a recognizable alternative to the parochial model of ministry, at least that is until the nineteenth century returned them. However, the significance of cathedrals not only survived the Reformation but was strengthened, often inheriting something of the monastic mantle. These self-governing institutions bound by a statute or rule, and committed to a liturgical round, have the potential to contribute something different and complementary within the fabric of Church life.

It is that distinctiveness which needs to be more clearly recognized in the contemporary Church. Cathedrals are not simply large parish churches exempt from contributing to diocesan funds. Potentially they are alternative ways of expressing the life of the Community of Faith which for that very reason can offer inspiration to a Church often experimenting and casting around for new directions. Yet, because cathedrals are part of the familiar ecclesiastical landscape it is easy for their potential to be overlooked even by, indeed most particularly by, those within the fold.

The nature of the Church of England is such that, as at this moment, each diocese has one church which is the bishop's seat and which is allocated a level of resources which is not available generally. That generous focusing of resources requires the assent of the whole Church. In these lean days the case continually has to be made for the validity of such a priority. The resources are channelled through the Church Commissioners in paying the stipend of a dean and two canons, as well as in contributing to the lay salaries of those cathedrals with little endowment or visitor income. Cathedrals are self-governing institutions, which means that they are also given, with the assent of the wider Church, room for manoeuvre, and can consequently develop an entrepreneurial flair. The result, at its best, is a focus for unity and community in every diocese, the potential to do liturgy well, a reflective and intelligent teaching ministry and a source for mission. Mission is typically extended through a visitor officer to tourists and pilgrims, through an education officer to literally thousands of schoolchildren and through an arts officer to the local cultural life. These officers are usually backed by an army of volunteers. Cathedrals are also able to provide a distinctive and visible presence that can relate to the fabric of local or regional society – civic, charitable, educational, media, business and commerce. Most cathedrals offer a shop and hospitality in a refectory. They are places to be, to meet and to feel the embrace of welcome without threat.

Within the total fabric of a Church which is having to restructure and downsize, and necessarily, therefore, going through a painful time, cathedrals are able to offer some encouragement. Cathedrals remain a point of growth and optimism, and are continuing to work on development strategies to cope with increased demands. It is true that the demands may be from tourists more often than pilgrims. Many children who visit are unclear about the Christian story and some of those who are touched by the arts performed in cathedrals may be uncertain searchers. For that very reason, cathedrals are at the interface of faith and secular indifference. To be there and to be buoyant is something the wider Church should value.

It is all too tempting for a stretched Church to want to behave like Samson bringing down the Philistine temple and its pillars on his own head and everybody else's. Why should cathedrals thrive at a difficult time? Why not at least level them down so that they suffer like the rest? These voices are to be heard even in the Church's highest councils. Cathedrals, therefore, need to tell their story, not to crow success, but so that the validity of what they are doing is recognized. The English Heritage survey undertaken jointly with the Association of English Cathedrals and published in June 2004 highlighted the good news. Cathedrals received more than 8.8 million visits in 2003. They generated additional local spending of £91 million with the total economic impact likely to be around £150 million. Over 12,000 people act as volunteers in cathedrals and 363,000 educational visits were made in 2003.[3]

All these varied activities bring to cathedrals a critical mass which enables them to be patrons of adventurous projects usually involving a concentration of skills beyond the ordinary, which makes them significant contributors to the national cultural life. It is a point often being pressed upon regional cultural consortia. The great Christian heritage of architecture, art, music and literature, which celebrates the image of God in humanity, is not simply a museum of the past. It remains a living, breathing reality for the present. *Les grands projets* can still be contemplated even in hard times. Great architectural statements, musical endeavour and artistic searchings are not completely abandoned to corporate money, civic enterprise or new wealth.

Human creativity grounded in the creativity of God finds a voice. Faith continues to speak through culture and to be generative of culture. Through its cathedrals it is possible for the Christian witness to present itself as part of the human story and its rich embrace of body, soul and spirit in the context of community and environment. Despite the huge and constant demands upon cathedrals to maintain their fabric, significant sums are invested in imaginative schemes that break new ground. More and more the imaginative use of stunning architectural space to speak to and welcome visitors and to involve children in a journey of discovery is evident. Wells Cathedral is a prime example with a 'Development Fund' underway to spend £5 million on conservation linked to developing new facilities to meet contemporary needs. Chelmsford Cathedral has raised £1.1 million in three phases to upgrade the facilities within the cathedral and to provide a Learning Centre for schools and adult education. Stunning refectories have been recently built at Salisbury and Norwich. Norwich writes of its £3.2 million development: 'The new refectory is a world class building and is our generation's contribution to the heritage of Norwich.'[4] They may be justly proud of the design by Hopkins Architects which slips a dancing combination of glass, limestone and oak into the sleeve of the existing medieval walls.

Canterbury Cathedral, as part of its service to the worldwide Anglican Communion, has built a magnificent, state-of-the-art, International Study Centre designed by Sir William Whitfield. It cost £12 million with auditorium, accommodation and dining space. Canterbury, with considerable justification, claims: 'The International Study Centre is the most important building erected in the Cathedral Precincts since the Reformation.'[5] The words give a context to an endeavour of our own generation.

Cathedrals are in a very good position to put together partnership funding packages. Lincoln Cathedral's £500,000 project to create an education and training centre involves also HLF (Heritage Lottery Fund), Lincolnshire Enterprise and Lincolnshire County Council. Birmingham Cathedral through partnership with the City Council has benefited from £3 million raised to regenerate the historic churchyard so as to landscape and transform a city-centre environment.

Liverpool Cathedral is seeking 'Objective One' funding from the European Union to part-fund a £2.5 million project to create a Visitor Centre and Visitor Experience.

The Millennium Commission, set up by Government to channel lottery funds to projects to celebrate the Millennium, has given awards to three cathedrals. Bradford's scheme for a multifaith centre in partnership with the City Council failed for lack of visitor numbers with a debt of £4.5 million. Although prizes are never awarded for failure, and one cannot underestimate the damage to small businesses of bad debt, it is worth pausing to contemplate the real risk involved in many projects undertaken by cathedrals. Cathedral projects are invariably launched in faith with no capital reserves. Christian faith ought to acknowledge the dignity of brave failure as well as the culture of success. The other two cathedrals to receive Millennium Commission funding were Southwark and St Edmundsbury.

Southwark Cathedral has, for £10.8 million, turned its face towards the Thames. The new buildings to the north of the cathedral church embrace the visitor with open arms. In contemporary architecture which resonates with history, the development provides refectory, shop, exhibition space, library, meeting rooms and other facilities. Southwark Cathedral's development lies alongside other South Bank projects including two that are also the responsibility of the Millennium Commission, namely, Tate Modern and the Millennium Footbridge. The Church of England through Southwark Cathedral has made a significant contribution to the partnership and cooperation which has opened up London's South Bank to a new generation of visitors.

St Edmundsbury Cathedral in Suffolk was able to commission a £12.3 million Millennium Project. It has involved the completion of the proposed design for the cathedral building itself. The task to give a medieval parish church, which became the cathedral for the new diocese of St Edmundsbury and Ipswich in 1914, enhanced architectural stature was undertaken by the architect Stephen Dykes Bower in the 1960s. The work broke off, conspicuously incomplete, awaiting a central tower, north transept and cloisters. The Millennium has enabled the outstanding work to be largely completed. The lantern tower is a significant addition to Suffolk's skyline and potentially a new county icon. In the words of the project Patron, His Royal Highness The Prince of Wales, it is: 'A spiritual beacon for the new Millennium.'

This author can speak authoritatively for only one project – the Millennium Project at Bury St Edmunds. What does it feel like to be involved in this particular and great work and to have some responsibility for unleashing a sum that runs into millions? You were aware that its conception was within swirling currents which may as likely carry you away as sweep you to destiny. There are risks and vulnerabilities for which the martyred and canonized young King Edmund is an appropriate patron. Opportunity often presents itself, and this was one of those occasions; grace was of its essence. A generous benefactor was the crucial factor. The Cathedral Architect Emeritus, Stephen Dykes Bower, died in 1994 at the age of 91. His commitment to a traditional Gothic solution to complete St Edmundsbury Cathedral led him to set up a trust from his estate which had benefited from his family's accumulated wealth. The trustees had to release the money, which after careful management amounted to £3 million, only if his vision were pursued. Their advisor was Stephen Dykes Bower's associate Warwick Pethers, who in the event became half of the architectural team working on the project. At the same time the Millennium Commission was now in existence. The National Lottery was still new, and suspicion in Church circles considerable. There was just a chance that to complete a cathedral for the Millennium might be attractive to the Commission, and would use the generosity of the architectural benefactor as a sort of lever to achieve considerably more. A county appeal would be needed to at least match the generosity of the benefactor but, as an element in the whole, would mean that its proceeds were effectively quadrupled.

'It nearly didn't happen!' sums up the coming to birth of the St Edmundsbury Project. The Millennium Commission turned down the first application based on existing plans. A second application with new plans had to be conceived and drawn up. To make a bid for funding of half of a £12 million project required detailed and expensive preparation. A seminar was set up which took place on 28 September 1996 chaired by Colin Amery, then Architectural Correspondent of the *Financial Times*, and now Chief Executive of the

135

World Monuments Fund; it gathered a wide spectrum of interested parties both regionally and nationally. The seminar concluded with a motion by His Grace the Duke of Grafton that all present were in support of a renewed application to the Commission. To fund the second application the cathedral congregation were invited to join a 300 club of people who would give £400 each immediately. That request was amazingly successful, with many people raiding their building society savings in a way they could ill afford. The responsibility upon the Dean when that further application was put on the remaindered list felt like the descent of a funeral pall. What had I done with those savings? I was summoned to the Millennium Commission and invited to withdraw the application. I remember stammering 'Why don't you shoot me? I don't see why I should take the initiative and withdraw.' The application stayed 'on the books' with only weeks left to run before the final Millennium Commission wave of applications concluded.

Meanwhile, a stunning and hitherto unseen (even by the Chapter) design solution for the tower by Hugh Mathew was published in *The Times* by Marcus Binney (*The Times* Architectural Correspondent) in July 1997. *Private Eye*, amazingly, at about the same time, took up the cudgels on behalf of the need for more spiritual projects to celebrate the Millennium. I cut both articles out and sent them to 10 Downing Street with a final appeal to the Millennium Commission. At the eleventh hour we were summoned to the Commission. As a result of a fruitful meeting, and working around the clock, the new design was submitted literally hours before the guillotine fell on the final Millennium Commission round. The award was announced in November 1997. A fax arrived early in the morning, and by lunchtime a press conference attended by senior Millennium Commission representatives had been arranged at the Angel Hotel, opposite the cathedral. The grant offer, 50 per cent of the total cost, was made subject to the capturing of the copyright within three months. Luckily the patience of the Millennium Commission stretched for the necessary eight months. The next task was to acquire the permissions from the Local Authority and, in place of Listed Building consent, also from the Cathedrals Fabric Commission in London and its local 'arm' known as the Fabric Advisory Committee. Not the tower, but the chimney for the boiler flue proved to be the controversial element! Project managers, quantity surveyors, engineers and builders had to be interviewed and appointed. Stonemasons needed to be identified and the appropriate stone sourced.

The County Appeal required its own structure, and without the support of the then Lord Lieutenant of Suffolk, Lord Belstead, who nominated the Appeal Chairman and the Appeal Director as well as attending many 'road shows', it would have been quite impossible. The emergence of two considerable benefactors gave the Appeal the headstart that it needed. Luckily the Cathedral Appeal anticipated other local millennium appeals and was deliberately launched in Ipswich, the county town, in May 1998, under the title of the Suffolk Cathedral Millennium Appeal. The conscious strategy of reminding the public that we are 'Suffolk's Cathedral' worked. Rather than being a drag, the Appeal became an opportunity to rove around Suffolk increasing the profile and identity of a fairly new cathedral as a county phenomenon. Venues were usually given and often food was provided. The county press was encouraging and supportive. The phenomenon of 'the Dome' seemed to work to our advantage. There was one hiccup: a 'Sporting Auction' to raise funds; the donated prizes included not only seats for Centre Court at Wimbledon but also lots for fishing and shooting. This brought a protest from the Animal Rights Movement. It made for an uncomfortable summer in 1999, and a wiser Dean at the end of it. The loyalty of some country folk was tested by this event and the decision to pull out, but I am gratified to say that, being Suffolk, it held.

Work began in December 1999 – catching the Millennium only by a hair's breadth. The build has lasted into its sixth year and involved almost 100 miles of scaffolding, 3,800 tons of stone and 600,000 bricks especially made for the project. Throughout, the relentless pursuit of perfection has been the standard set by the architectural team. There have been precarious moments to challenge architects and engineers. These have included the interface of old and new-build, the assessing of the strength of the existing structures and the challenge of design solutions for the complex scaffolding let alone the Gothic tower. The dense scaffolding shrouded in mystery by protective sheeting could have won the Turner Prize. It had all the elements of complexity, majesty, sculptural beauty, incongruity in a Gothic project, and abandoned bridges as the structure grew upwards and sloughed its most recent umbilical lifeline linking hoist to developing embryo. The stonework has often reminded me of Solomon's Temple for which, similarly, the stone was shaped at the quarry and then brought to site ready to assemble: 'The house was built with stone finished at the quarry, so that neither hammer nor axe nor any tool of iron was heard in the temple while it was being built' (1 Kings 6.7). The painstaking accuracy of all involved so that complex shapes of stone arrive and Lego-like slot into place is almost superhuman. To sustain that sort of discipline over a period of years by a team of people, many still in their youth, requires a stamina which it is difficult to articulate. It has to be about pride in work and not about the incentives of piecework. Entrepreneurial flair, drive, hands-on ability and a dash of canniness on the part of the masonry contractor delivered Barnack stone, thought to be unavailable for almost 500 years, at a price that was able to compete with the necessary European-wide tendering process. Interestingly the stonemason's other major works included the Islamic Studies Centre at Oxford University, making some interesting juxtapositions at the stonemason's yard. The Oxford project, too, shared the same royal patron.

The brick laying was a separate contractor's package and so required significant cooperation for a seamless task to be achieved. I have preached about the bricklayer who, remarkably and in the full glare of the television cameras, trained The Prince of Wales to lay the foundation bricks of the first buttress. Although people may extol the stonework for a thousand years, the brickwork at the core of the tower which carries much of its strength will be invisible. It has been done with lime mortar and not cement which is a wholly different ballgame and has to be rigorously accurate otherwise the pre-cut stone will not bond to it. It is a work of the inner chamber – 'your Father who sees in secret will reward you [openly]' (Matthew 6.6). The contractors are a major public company, they have to deliver a profit for their shareholders, yet their impressive local team ('the first eleven') has consistently prioritized the task. So often, when there has been a delay or a problem they have searched for a way around it. If you asked any person working on the project to explain what they were doing they would have answered 'completing a cathedral'.

The concentration of craftsmanship may be appropriately described as 'awesome'. Some have cut their teeth or served their apprenticeship on the project. The translation of exquisite plans into reality by people with skills that have survived generations is humbling. The project has involved stonemasons, bricklayers, plasterers, plumbers, glaziers, carpenters, flintworkers and blacksmiths. Seeing a keystone being slotted into an arch, like the slice of a cake being replaced, or the completion of the first flint panel of an 'E' for Edmund surmounted by a crown does have something of being present at the moment of creation about it.

There is, of course, also the human factor to every project. Any team assembled from professionals, businessmen, craftsmen and a thankfully irrepressible volunteer Cathedral Project Co-ordinator will not be without its tensions. Any such varied team would give different answers to the question: 'At what point does painstaking craftsmanship become obsession and economically unsustainable?' Those differing answers had to be held together by the stamina of the ever-optimistic Project Manager, as well as painstakingly negotiated with West-Country charm by the client's persistent and dedicated Quantity Surveyor. Another question arises: 'Who is the client?' The Dean and Chapter thought they were, but what about the Millennium Commission and, indeed, what about the legacy of Stephen Dykes Bower which triggered everything in the first place and which came with a specific architectural brief and trustees to watch over it? The stakeholders in a cathedral project are complex, and the wisdom of Solomon sometimes in all too short supply.

This vignette of ten years devoted to the Suffolk Cathedral Millennium Project needs summing up. It inspired me to write a book of prayers to celebrate its completion, despite the times of trial. Something deep in me quite genuinely resonated to what was going on within the boundaries of the site even when access to that site for the client could seem like the search for the Holy Grail. It was a project robust, yet very vulnerable to economic logic and finance, to the availability of materials, to the pace of architectural solutions, to unexpected problems and to frail humanity. It was a project solidly physical, involving pulleys, brawn and muscle, cranes, ashlars and helmets. A great vat of liquid lime mortar was constantly brewed, stirred and tested by the 'head chef'. The shrill sound of bricks being accurately sawn to shape was insistent rather than musical. Yet the physical was soaked in spirituality, in commitment, endeavour, painful self-discipline and an inner thirst for the truest and the best. These were not medieval builders rushing to Mass – though the cathedral prayers somehow daily fitted around the blows of the mason's mallet. Yet, these were men whose lasting achievements are prayers in stone before the throne of heaven.

Les grands projets need theological justification. That justification is to be found in reflection upon God as creator and the significance of global and environmental issues. Much of the process of seeking 'new ways of being Church' is looking for cells that separate themselves out in a very specific way from the local community and carry a very distinct and defined identity. In terms of giving an account of the faith that is in them they have enormous strength, but in terms of relating to the structures of society and the processes of creation they are often weak. There need to be voices from within the life of faith reminding Christians that they are not simply 'Jesus people', but an Easter community with a Trinitarian faith. In a recent *Times* leader, the writer took up a comment from the Bishop of Manchester that the established Church is in danger of becoming a minority sect. It concluded in a very upbeat way for cathedrals. It said:

> The exceptions are the great cathedrals, which are remarkably successful in remaining at the heart of their cities, attracting visitors, worshippers and cash and spreading their influence far beyond their precincts. They should lead the churches' fight to remain a vibrant part of Britain's life.[6]

If cathedrals are a source of strength for the Church's future, then it must be partly to do with their scale, their place as regional symbols, their being part of the landscape. They are there for everybody, they relate to their cities and their counties and to the structures of society. They span the generations and their stones speak of geological time. The strength of a cathedral is its ability to witness to God not as simply private and domestic but as Creator. As bishops signal the universal and manage the interface between Church and society, so does the seat of the bishop.

'Small is beautiful' is a guide when appropriate but not a dogma. Reality is more complex than a single insight. That complexity, in a way appropriate to this discussion, is tackled in the Old Testament in its juxtaposition of *tent* and *Temple*. Sometimes *Temple* is popularly interpreted as the shadow side of *tent* in its Old Testament context. The latter is how we should be: small-scale, provisional, flexible and moving on. The former represents what we want to be: grandiose, fixed and immovable. But, that is simply a misunderstanding. Instead *tent* and *Temple* set up a dynamic tension in the Old Testament, and any attempt to dissolve the tensions is to miss the point.

There is an importance in Israel being recalled to her former identity, not least in the attitude to strangers in her midst: 'A wandering Aramean was my ancestor; he went down into Egypt and lived there as an alien' (Deuteronomy 26.5). But the hymn book of the Temple, the book of Psalms, claims our attention also in celebrating the scale of the Creator's work: 'The heavens are telling the glory of God; and the firmament proclaims his handiwork' (Psalm 19.1). We need to know God as Father in the bosom of the nomadic family, but we need also to honour God as King, to let heaven's arches ring and sense creation hushed in awe.

In a world that is now recognized as a global village – interconnected and interdependent – there need to be symbols that can speak of that truth. 'No man is an island'. Nothing is simply local, but every event or action has a profound impact on other peoples and on the environment. Temples have in the biblical tradition been part of that order of witness. We are used to the idea that medieval congregations who were not literate might nonetheless 'read' the story of Christ and the saints from the stained glass and the murals of the churches. In the same way the populace of ancient Judea could 'read' the significance of their Temple. For pilgrims to Jerusalem, the Temple witnessed silently but clearly to God as Creator and to a cosmos with an equilibrium dependent upon order and justice. It is likely that both of the two great creation stories that open the book of Genesis were 'read' from the Jerusalem Temple. They are reflections on the Temple witness by Israel's intellectuals.

The Temple was built as a royal palace to celebrate the kingship of God. As *Father* is related to family and tent, so *King* is related to order and cosmos. God was celebrated as King in the building of a Temple to articulate his ruling over and control of the unruly primeval waters which had been driven back to secure the stability of creation. A specific numinous place could gather and express that wealth of insight.

A temple in the Old Testament could relate the local to the global and mediate a universal context. The reality of that we meet in the New Testament in the description of the day of Pentecost in the Acts of the Apostles. The Temple, as a place of pilgrimage, had gathered into itself representatives from across the known world: 'Parthians, Medes, Elamites, and residents of Mesopotamia, Judea and Cappadocia, Pontus and Asia, Phrygia and Pamphylia, Egypt and the parts of Libya belonging to Cyrene, and visitors from Rome . . . Cretans and Arabs . . .' (Acts 2.9–11a). The Temple would certainly tangibly demonstrate its universal credentials at the time of a festival.

Something of the mantle of the Temple falls upon our churches. As they gather their communities around them and themselves melt into the landscape they signal something organic and related. Inasmuch as cathedrals are especially charged with clothing themselves with the identity of Temple they signal strongly an environmental and cosmic perspective, they witness to scale, to the global significance of small actions and to the integrity of creation that is harmed by injustice. All this is focused within the limited boundaries of very specific sacred space. That insight was tangibly brought home to me on the one occasion that I visited one of the quarries from which stone was being sourced to be built into St Edmundsbury Cathedral. It was something of a moonscape; I saw great boulders blasted from the wounded earth where they had belonged for millions of years. That geological time, tamed and shaped, becomes a cathedral.

Cathedrals locate human beings firmly on the side of the creature, but as part of a wonderful and complex order. They lead the creature, like Job, to admit, 'I have uttered what I did not understand, things too wonderful for me, which I did not know' (Job 42.3). Perhaps our own generation is recovering the ability to read a building and interpret the meaning that it signals which can be more eloquent than words.

In a way that seems to be more and more crucial to the modern quest for the spiritual, cathedrals can offer a transforming experience. If religion appeals to duty, it seems spirituality must deliver a tangible personal intuition – 'the tug of silver'.[7] Cathedrals welcome the visitor, whether as worshipper, wanderer or the indifferent perplexed, and they deliver an experience. That experience may be about height, depth, colour, sound, scale, space, history or story. The sheer scale of things, the beauty of holiness, the rumour of faith, the drifting tones of evensong from remote choir stalls scarcely discernible, all allow the skirts of mystery to be touched. For a moment, people for whom too close a definition of what is happening would turn their wonderment to ashes may know the spiritual. All this has been captured by Ronald Blythe when he refers to cathedrals and the 'old-new numinosity'.[8] *Les grands projets* are part of that mission and that order of thinking.

Cathedrals also witness to something beyond our experience and place us in a greater context. It is not fanciful to sense in the multi-lingual literature at the cathedral door, in the exhibition about Fair Trade, in the prayers which gather concerns from across the globe left by the candle stand, in the resonances of regional celebrations and in the scale of the building – in all this it is not fanciful to sense the call of the universal creator. The God and Father of Our Lord Jesus Christ finds witness in the hewn stone, in the smell of the herbs in the monks' garden, in the play of light in the cloister, in the record of the generations and the word of greeting at the threshold. Doors of wonder are opened by walking into a cathedral. That is the ultimate justification for these great projects.

Notes

1 Exemplified by E. F. Schumacher, *Small Is Beautiful* (London, Blond & Briggs, 1973).
2 Antonia Gransden, 'The Cult of St Mary at Beodricsworth and then in Bury St Edmunds Abbey to *c.* 1150', *Journal of Ecclesiastical History*, vol. 52, no. 4 (October 2004) (653).

3 'The Economic and Social Impact of Cathedrals in England' (June 2004), ECOTEC Research and Consulting Ltd.

4 Henry Cator, Chairman, Norwich Cathedral Campaign, *Update* (Summer 2004).

5 *About our Centre* (Canterbury Cathedral International Study Centre, distributed 2004).

6 Leading Article, *The Times* (20 March 2004).

7 A phrase used by Isobel Thrilling in the poem 'Lumber', *The Chemistry of Angels* (Kingston upon Hull, Halfacrown Press, 2000).

8 Ronald Blythe, 'Word from Wormingford', *Church Times* (26 March 2004). Referring to cathedrals, Ronald Blythe writes: 'Crowds of worshippers, for cathedrals, have become part of the old-new numinosity, and their lovely services a great attraction. Amos would not have hurled his wrath at them and their singing feasts, but would have joined in the processional.'

11

A post-script: The place of cathedrals in the religious life of Europe

GRACE DAVIE

In this short post-script, I consider the place of cathedrals in the religious economy of Europe (more especially Northern Europe) as this is emerging in the early years of the twenty-first century. The material contained in these chapters enables a better understanding of the relative popularity of cathedrals, not only in Britain but also elsewhere.

Two things are happening at once in the religious life of Europe. The fact that they have occurred at the same time is partly a coincidence; each, however, encourages the other. On the one hand, the historic churches – despite their continuing presence – are losing their capacity to discipline the religious thinking of large sections of the population (especially among the young). At the same time, the range of choice widens all the time as new forms of religion come into Europe from outside, largely as the result of the movement of people. Populations that have arrived in Europe primarily for economic reasons bring with them different ways of being religious (some Christian and some not); conversely European people travel the world, experiencing among other things considerable religious diversity. In this sense a genuine religious market is emerging in most parts of the continent.[1]

The crucial question lies, however, not in the existence of the market in itself but in the capacities of Europeans to make use of this. Hence the significance of an increasingly observable trend which is taking place both inside and outside the historic churches – from an understanding of religion as a form of obligation to an increasing

145

emphasis on 'consumption' or choosing. What until moderately recently was simply imposed (with all the negative connotations of this word) or inherited (a rather more positive spin) becomes instead a matter of personal choice. I go to church (or to another religious organization) because I want to, maybe for a short period or maybe for longer, to fulfil a particular rather than a general need in my life and where I will continue my attachment so long as it provides what I want, but I have no *obligation* either to attend in the first place or to continue if I don't want to.

As such this pattern is entirely compatible with the (traditional) parish model: the churches need to be there in order that I may attend them if I so choose. The 'chemistry', however, gradually changes, a shift which is discernible in both practice and belief, not to mention the connections between them. There is, for example, a clearly observable change in the patterns of confirmation in the Church of England. Everyone knows that the overall number of confirmations has dropped dramatically in the post-war period, evidence once again of institutional decline. In England, though not yet in the Nordic countries, confirmation is no longer a teenage rite of passage, but a relatively rare event undertaken as a matter of personal choice by people of all ages. Hence a marked rise in the proportion of adult confirmations among the candidates as a whole – up to 40 per cent by the mid-1990s (by no means enough, however, to offset the fall among teenagers).

Confirmation becomes, therefore, a very significant event for the individuals who choose this option, an attitude that is bound to affect the rite itself – which now includes the space for a public declaration of faith. It becomes in fact an opportunity to make public what has often been an entirely private activity. It is increasingly common, moreover, to baptize an adult candidate immediately before the confirmation, an action which is evidence in itself of the fall in infant baptism some 20 to 30 years earlier. Taken together, these events indicate a marked change in the nature of membership in the historic churches which become, in some senses, much more like their non-established counterparts. Voluntarism (a market) is beginning to establish itself de facto, regardless of the constitutional position of the churches. Or, to continue the chemical analogy a little further, a whole set of new reactions are set off which in the *longer* term (the stress is important) may have a profound effect on traditional patterns of religious activity.

So far the trends are considerably more visible in some parts of Europe than in others. There is, for instance, a marked parallel between Anglicans and the Catholic Church in France in this respect: adult baptisms in the Church of England match very closely those in France[2] – indeed the similarity in the statistics is almost uncanny given the very different ecclesiologies embodied in the two Churches (one Catholic and one Protestant). But it is precisely this shift across very different denominations that encourages the notion that something profound is taking place. The Lutherans, however – despite their reputation for being the most secular countries in Europe, still stick to a more traditional pattern as far as confirmation is concerned, though the manner in which they do this is changing. Large numbers of young people now choose the option of a confirmation camp rather than a series of weekly meetings.[3] In making this choice, confirmation becomes an 'experience' in addition to a rite of passage, implying a better fit with other aspects of youth culture.

The stress on experience is important in other ways as well. It can be seen in the choices that the religiously active appear to be making at least in the British case. Here, within a constituency which is evidently reduced, two options stand out as disproportionately popular. The first is the conservative evangelical church – the success story of late twentieth-century churchgoing, both inside and outside the mainstream. These are churches which draw their members from a relatively wide geographical area and work on a congregational rather than parish model. Individuals are invited to opt in rather than opt out, and membership implies commitment to a set of specified beliefs and behavioural codes. For significant numbers of people, these churches offer firm boundaries, clear guidance and considerable support – effective protection from the vicissitudes of life. (They run the risk, of course, of the corresponding negative attributes; more than other types of churches, they can become both excluding and exclusive.)

This is not the whole story, however. On closer inspection, it is clear that some kinds of evangelical church are doing better than others – those that incorporate a charismatic element. Old-fashioned biblicism is noticeably less popular. It is the softer charismatic forms of evangelicalism that appeal in particular to late modern populations, a suggestion strongly supported by the findings of the Kendal project.[4] The tendency is wonderfully epitomized in the Alpha Course – a formula which brings together basic biblical teaching, warm friendship and an emphasis on the Holy Spirit. Clearly this is a winning combination; the success rates are impressive by any conventional indicator (geographical spread, the numbers of classes, throughput of customers and a growing profile in the population at large).[5] Whether you like Alpha or not (and many people, both inside and outside the churches, do not), it is hard to think of an equivalent movement, religious or secular, of parallel proportions.

Very different and much less frequently recognized in the scholarly writing about religion in modern Britain is the growing popularity of cathedrals. Hence the importance of this book. Cathedrals, and their equivalents, deal with diverse and not always compatible constituencies – a point repeatedly stressed in the preceding chapters. Working from the inside out, they are frequented by regular and irregular worshippers, pilgrims, visitors and tourists, bearing in mind that the lines between these groups are frequently blurred. The numbers, moreover, are considerable – the more so on special occasions, both civic and religious. Hence the concerns about upkeep and facilities which lead in turn to difficult debates about finance, about ownership and access, about conservation and innovation. The same, of course, is true of the pilgrim sites all over Europe. As the numbers of pilgrims continue to rise right across the continent, the wear and tear on the infrastructure is correspondingly increased.

Is it possible to explain the relative popularity of cathedrals in terms of a model of consumption? Here this book is helpful. Cathedrals offer a distinctive product – one which includes traditional liturgy, top-class music and excellence in preaching, all of which take place in a historic and often very beautiful building, an important repository of individual and collective memory. Above all, a visit to a cathedral is an aesthetic experience, sought after by a wide variety of people, including those for whom membership or commitment presents difficulties. Cathedrals are places where there is no obligation to opt in or to participate in communal activities beyond the service itself. In this respect, they become almost the mirror image of the evangelical churches already described.

What then is the common feature in these very different stories? It is, I think, the experiential or 'feel-good' factor, whether this be expressed in charismatic worship, in the Alpha weekend, in the tranquillity of cathedral evensong or in a special cathedral occasion (a candlelit carol service or a major civic event). The point is that we *feel* something; we *experience* the sacred, the set apart. The purely cerebral is less appealing. Émile Durkheim – a founding father of modern sociology – was entirely correct in this respect. It is the taking part that matters for late modern populations and the feelings so engendered. If we feel nothing, we are much less likely either to be attracted in the first place or to come back for more.

Interestingly, exactly the same combination of choices has been identified by a leading sociologist of religion in France. In her book *Le pèlerin et le convert*,[6] Danièle Hervieu-Léger identifies two ways of being religious in late modernity: the pilgrim and the convert. The book, in fact, is part of a larger scheme of writing in which Hervieu-Léger describes the collapse of the traditional model of religious life in France, but not the collapse of religiousness per se.[7] Privileging the French case, Hervieu-Léger singles out the pilgrim (the seeker) and the convert (the decision-maker) as the role models for the twenty-first century. No longer is it possible to be simply a Catholic or not – in French terminology to be a *pratiquant* or a *non-pratiquant*. Most people are neither as the lines between practice and non-practice are crossed and recrossed all the time. With this in mind, the cathedral, both in this country and in France, offers an attractive option in the religious economy of Northern Europe. Cathedrals and those who work in them have everything to play for.

I will end on a personal note. From 2000 to 2001, I spent the academic year in Sweden – more precisely at the University of Uppsala, where I attended the cathedral on many occasions. One event in particular stands out: a performance of Arvo Pärt's *Requiem*. Technically speaking this was a concert, in the sense that the public paid to go in, but the line between concert and liturgy was necessarily fine given the nature of the work and the place of performance. How then were we to categorize the event? Given that the cathedral was full to capacity in a country in which churchgoing is notoriously low, it seems sensible to conclude that most people thought they were going to a concert. But the 'experience' indicated otherwise. Here was sacred music on sacred ground, performed to the highest possible standard – a combination constantly replicated in cathedrals all over Europe. Where else?

Notes

1 Some sort of market has, of course, been in existence for decades if not centuries (since the acceptance de facto of religious toleration). In the later post-war decades, however, it has vastly extended.
2 See Grace Davie, *Religion in Modern Europe: A Memory Mutates* (Oxford: Oxford University Press, 2000), pp. 71–2.
3 This information came from a Swedish colleague – Per Pettersson. Dr Pettersson also remarked on the *increasing* proportion of young Finns who are opting for confirmation.
4 For more information about the Kendal project, see <http://www.lancs.ac.uk/depts/ieppp/kendal/book.htm> and P. Heelas and L. Woodhead, *The Spiritual Revolution: Why Religion Is Giving Way to Spirituality* (Oxford: Blackwell, 2005).
5 See S. Hunt, *The Alpha Enterprise: Evangelism in a Post-Christian Era* (London: Ashgate, 2004), for a very fair account of Alpha.
6 Paris, Flammarion 1999.
7 See in particular Danièle Hervieu-Léger, *Catholicisme, la fin d'un monde* (Paris, Bayard, 2003).

12

The future

CHRISTOPHER LEWIS

The picture of cathedrals given here is one of hope based on experience. In an age when religion around the world is exploding and diverse, Christianity in Western Europe appears less active, in terms of church attendance if not of belief. At the same time, there are struggles going on within the Church as to what vision of Christianity is to be to the fore. Pentecostalism is rising worldwide in both its more experientialist and fundamentalist forms,[1] and much of the liveliness of the Church in Western Europe is provided in charismatic churches, most prominently among immigrants but also in communities of people who have been in Europe much longer. Such churches are for the consciously converted, gatherings of the like-minded to worship and to spread the word to others. Although now often more conscious of obligations to the poor and suffering, the model is of a self-contained assembly of the saved.

Is there another model? It is the contention here that there is, articulated in some churches and especially in cathedrals. If the gathered churches have the ark as their picture or even at times the circle of wagons, the alternative is of sacred space or common ground on which Christians meet to worship but which is at the same time a place for all. How about the model of the fried egg, with its defined centre yet indefinite edges? Here the lack of the definition of the boundary is as important as the definition of the centre: the whole is specifically outward looking and evangelistic in the sense of providing a threshold which it is not hard to cross. That such a model must be concerned with the issues and most particularly with the tragedies of the world should follow, for unless it does that it will degenerate into an institution merely concerned with its own continuation. A Church that follows the Jesus of Good Friday cannot attend to its survival as a high priority, for it will lose its soul.

Any turning to Christ demands self-examination and the plea to God that he will forgive and renew us. So the claims made in this book are coupled to a challenge thrown out to cathedrals and other churches. The best way of spelling out the challenge is to see how cathedrals may appear to those who approach them and then turn away or to those who merely pass by. Given the fact that the boundary between Church and world is so crucial for an understanding of the Church, cathedrals pay far too much attention to those who come and too little to those who do not.

Cathedrals as sinister

'That's a great dark place; I've never been in.' Visitors to cathedrals tend to like them, which is not surprising for they have taken a decision at least to wander around. Yet, what of the perspective of those who avoid them? Cathedrals are the work of the devil: great cumbersome dominating piles, full of menace and overflowing gutters, the wind whistling round them. 'It is always windy around cathedrals.' Many cathedrals were built by near-slave labour in order to symbolize the triumph of secular and religious powers, towering above a conquered people. And, if you somehow penetrate inside, there is a forest of pillars, a mausoleum to the rich, full of the incomprehensible symbols of a remote religion obsessed with death, surrounded by cavernous passages occasionally populated by supercilious people in black robes. Whether moved on or included in, in neither state do you belong. You might as well be in the forested atrium of one of those towering office blocks in the City of London, guarded by blondes and bent on its obscure high-financial purposes, wanting nothing of you. The message is much the same: whatever the ideals with which this institution started, it lost the vision long ago and instead has built a castle for its own glorification and for the exclusion of those who do not like its definition of the way the world is. If its 'take' on reality needs walls as thick as this to protect it, little wonder that people vote for the great outdoors.

And the gates of this Chapel were shut,
And 'Thou shalt not' writ over the door;
So I turn'd to the Garden of Love
That so many sweet flowers bore;

And I saw it was filled with graves,
And tomb-stones where flowers should be;
And Priests in black gowns were walking their rounds,
And binding with briars my joys and desires.[2]

Nobody who wants to work in cathedrals should do so. No, that must be wrong, but it is not far wrong. For the temptation of those who want total immersion in a large religious institution is that they will lose hold of Jesus in a year or perhaps two, much though Jesus would like to keep hold of them. As in other areas of life, the lure of regularity, status and the beauty and power of large buildings is just too great for mortals to resist.

If you start with Jesus, you might get a number of different patterns of life, but you certainly would not get cathedrals. Yet cathedrals appear to work for the Christian faith, if steered with attention to the guidance of the Holy Spirit and therefore to the avoidance of the numerous pitfalls they present. The paradox summed up in those two sentences is the subject of this book. Something is going on here which has its dark and dangerous side, yet there is mystery and truth here too.

Cathedrals as sacred spaces

Take a more pagan picture of the cathedral. Here is a sacred place and space, probably (the archaeologists will tell us) built on top of other efforts to experience and placate the divine. The Christians came along and recycled the building materials and indeed the place as well, giving it a style of their own. It is still, however, a sacred grove in which smell and touch and colour define the sacred place just as much as walls and floor and roof define it. So we may come in and be quiet (or even quite noisy) and dance a bit, light a candle, pray to the infinite, meditate and wonder what all the symbols mean: green men and crosses, masons' marks and liturgical colours. Some will see the place as a mystical space and nobody will correct them unless they tip over into blacker arts.

There was once a notice in a derelict area of London which read 'Creation of an open space'. In a way that is ironic, for it is human beings who have overrun the open spaces and now need to reclaim them. The notice makes the point, however, that in a world which has been taken over by us we need to work hard at spaces and indeed to create them. The same is true of sacred spaces. The test case for the way in which they are created is how the boundaries are controlled. In fact the test case is much more specific than that: how easy is it for the person who is disturbed or distressed to enter, and what happens to them when they do? For the Church, the treatment of those coming from the margins is crucial.

A young man entered a cathedral in great distress. The first thing he noticed was the prayer board, covered in all kinds of requests to God. He took a pencil and wrote on a slip: 'I am so sorry for what has happened. I would do anything to change it. You did not deserve it at all. It was all my fault. I'm sorry. All my love [and then his name].' He found someone passing by and asked to be shown how to pray. It transpired later that he had knocked over and killed a man while driving his car.

Another man in the same cathedral has a history of mental illness and spends much of his day sitting in the building or walking around it, occasionally attending a service. He is one of the 'odd' people who often frequent cathedrals, sometimes frightening visitors but usually quiet and happy to be in a safe and warm place, full of mystery.

Those are test cases. In Western Europe this is not an age of institutions, yet perhaps for that very reason some institutions work for people, for they need them. And it is strange that, contrary to all the predictions, a high percentage of people see themselves as 'spiritual' and have aspirations to lead spiritual lives. There are millions of people who start sentences: 'I am not religious but . . .'

The future

In spite of the plain evidence of spiritual belief and activity, shown for example in the European Values Study, the dominant theory among academics and the media is one of inevitable religious decline. That is a simple model, inherited from a time 30 or 40 years ago when the figures for churchgoing seemed to point that way. The result is that a large and influential group in society is closed to what may as a matter of fact be happening; they just do not give religion space because the evidence does not fit easily into their view of the world. The sociologist and theologian David Martin gives a vivid illustration of the persistence of a particular perception in face of the facts:

> The power of the ruling paradigms came home to me most forcibly on a bus full of Western academics in Guatamala. When told that 66 per cent of the population was Catholic they asked no questions about where the rest might be, even though the answer shouted at them from texts on huts in remote El Peten, storehouse churches called 'Prince of Peace', and buses announcing 'Jesus is coming'.[3]

In other words, the theorists were unable to see the plain signs of Pentecostal religion which were there in front of their eyes.

In Europe the signs of the times are harder to read, but there is little doubt, except perhaps in the quarters mentioned above, that we are not turning out strictly rationalistic post-Enlightenment people. Religious life has been, as it were, deregulated but is nevertheless alive in a somewhat diffuse and disorganized way. The institutions are in trouble and yet are somehow expected to carry the memory for many: 'say one for me'.

Given this bazaar of spiritual values, the natural tendency is for the Christian churches to emphasize their distinctiveness and get their wagons in a circle. The alternative is more risky but is the one which we endorse here. What will be the main features for the future in the churches and cathedrals which choose an open model?

First, the cathedrals will need to keep their comparative independence from the rest of the Church. The fact that they are self-governing and that many of them have a degree of financial autonomy means that they can take risks which other parts of the Church are less able to do. The result can be spectacular failure on the one hand, but on the other there can be imaginative projects and experiments (alongside everyday worship and prayer) which are of use to the whole Church.

So, second, there will be real flair in a number of areas of religious life: in bold ecumenical and interfaith initiatives, some of which will undoubtedly be controversial in the Church at large; in liturgical ventures which combine high standards with real creativity; in prayer which captures the imagination; in music-making which uses the best in the service of God; in building projects which enhance the cathedrals' role as places of welcome and evangelism; in educational work which catches the imagination and shows children and adults paths to travel beyond themselves to God; in strange new liaisons with secular institutions; in artistic commissions that demonstrate a continuation of the great tradition of religious art; in involvement with justice issues which keep the Church facing outwards and caring about the life of the world.

The list above sounds like an activist checklist, but need not be that, for it is drawn together by the wish to be a sacred place open to all, reaching out to many and with daily prayer and worship at its core. New ways of being the Church are both presented by the society we live in and also created by the Christian community itself. The third feature of the future may therefore be to discover new ways of 'belonging' which are neither the free-floating network nor the settled community but have features of both. That model of belonging presents to cathedrals criteria for self-examination and an ideal to be pursued under God. Here is a role both on the edge of the Church and at its centre.

Notes

1 See Harvey Cox, *Fire from Heaven* (London, Cassell, 1996).
2 William Blake, 'The Garden of Love', from his *Songs of Experience*, in, e.g., *William Blake* (Harmondsworth, Penguin, 1958).
3 David Martin, 'Personal Reflections in the Mirror of Halevy and Weber', in R. Fenn (ed.), *The Blackwell Companion to the Sociology of Religion* (Oxford, Blackwell, 1991, pp. 23–38 (27), quoted in Grace Davie, *Europe – the Exceptional Case* (London, Darton, Longman and Todd, 2002), p. 75.

Index